This masterpiece has been created by me.

Nobody helped me do it.

It is

M Y S C R A P B O O K

Signed
Mr Bear (A.R. R.A.C.T.S.B.)

My friend, Mr. Tippy-Tap-Tap-Rat-Tat-Tap-Ting!

One

Written by Robin Driscoll
with Richard Curtis and Andrew Clifford

HarperCollinsPublishers
25 Ryde Road, Pymble, Sydney NSW 2073,
Australia
31 View Road, Glenfield, Auckland 10,
New Zealand

First published in Australia in 1997
by HarperCollins*Publishers* Pty Limited
ACN 009 913 517
A member of the HarperCollins*Publishers*
(Australia) Pty Limited Group

Copyright © 1997 Robin Driscoll and Richard Curtis
Film stills © PolyGram Filmed Entertainment

This book is copyright.
Apart from any fair dealing for the purposes of private study,
research, criticism or review, as permitted under the Copyright Act,
no part may be reproduced by any process without written
permission. Inquiries should be addressed to the publishers.

National Library of Australia Cataloguing-in-Publication data:
Driscoll, Robin.
Bean: the scrapbook
ISBN 0 7322 6177 5
1. Bean (Motion picture). I. Curtis, Richard. II. Atkinson, Rowan. III. Title. 791.4372

Printed in Hong Kong

987654321 97 98 99

Picture credits

AFP/PA News: page 30
Nigel Davies: pages 63 bottom right; 85 bottom; 89 bottom
Network Photographers: page 75
PolyGram/Pictorial Press: page 79
Topham/Press Association: page 75
Wallace Collection, London/Bridgeman Art Library, London: page 69
The paintings depicted in the postcards on pages 87, 88 & 89 hang in the National Gallery
All film stills by Liam Daniel, Suzanne Hanover and Melissa Moseley
Drawings and all other photographs by Robin Driscoll

Every effort has been made to contact all copyright holders. In case of error, please write
to the publisher to ensure a full acknowledgement in future editions.

Designed by Nigel Davies
Page photography by Derek Askem

Handwritten note:

Shopping list for my holiday
Underpants x 2
Soap x 2
Toothpaste (mint) x 1
Cotton Buds x 100
Socks x 2
Suncream 6 gallons
Sunglasses x 1

OOOOH, How Hoity Toity!

Two

C O N T E N T S

(Wait and see, tee, hee, hee...)

If you wear reading glasses
now is the time to put them on!

me

Me by me

EARTH is a rather difficult planet to live on I find. Especially my bit of it (which is: c/o Mrs. Wicket, 'Daffodils', 12 Arbor Road, Highbury, London N10, England). No matter what I do, every day turns out to be more of a torment than the day before. It's only since I recently decided to put some of my very important thoughts and experiences on paper, for the benefit of mankind, that I have come closer to understanding why my every waking hour is spent pushing poo up hill with a pointed stick. This affliction, I am certain, can only be due to my having to share this planet with very, very, STUPID people. You just would not believe how many STUPID-HEADS there are cluttering up the place; all sorts of queer fish, I can tell you.

① Appendix at back of book

Of course, I do not number you, oh brainy reader (or BRAINY-HEAD), among these dunces. Oh no. If I may try to be charitable for a moment; I believe the good Lord put us all here for a specific purpose. It's just that everybody else's specific purpose seems to be to get under my feet and make my life a ruddy MISERY day in and day out.

David by me.

Everybody that is except a nice man I know called David Langley, who I had the delightful good fortune of staying with on a recent visit to California. (That's in AMERICA for any STUPID-HEADS who might be reading this by accident. If that means YOU I suggest you give this book to someone who is NOT stupid and save us all a lot of time and mucking about.) ② Appendix at back of book

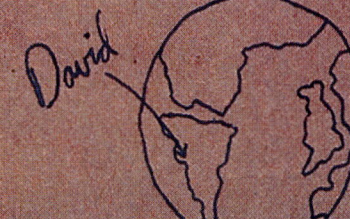
David

Five

David Langley is the most agreeable and brilliant person I have ever met. He speaks quite highly of me, as it happens, which is rather odd considering that, during my short stay with him and his excellent family, I caused them absolutely no end of irreversible damage.

David and his family

But more about my best friend, David, later. For now I shall start my very interesting story at the beginning. I'll keep going till I get to the middle, then go on, and on, and on, all the way to THE END. I've seen this technique used quite satisfactorily in other great works of literature which is an AMAZING coincidence, I think.

I adored this great masterpiece, especially pages 1, 2, 3, 4, 5, 31, 82 and 1315. Ruddy marvellous!

Six

'T H E B E G I N N I N G'

(N.B. For STUPID-HEADS:
The beginning starts NOW!)

My mini and I were late for work and Knightsbridge was one big enormous traffic jam. Very, very, inconvenient, obviously. All the dim drivers just would not get weaving! I'm no expert but if these blear-eyed laggards simply stayed in bed for another half hour in the mornings they'd save those of us, with important jobs to get to, a tremendous amount of trouble, tsk! tsk! (H.M. Government please take note).

My mini by me

Seven

③ Appendix at be- oh, you know that by now!

I got to work only five minutes late that day which was excellent because my job is the most IMPORTANT job in the Royal National Gallery IF NOT THE WORLD. It's not as easy as some people might think. We have to be on the lookout for all sorts of threats to the paintings, you know. I keep an incredibly close eye on the ones in my room but there is one problem I just can't overcome: people coming in and LOOKING at them. Really! I have sent our Chairman, Lord Walton, countless memos suggesting that I be given a gun, and be locked up alone with the paintings, thus keeping so-called art lovers at a safe distance. (I heard nothing from His Lordship on the subject until one day, Delilah, His secretary, let slip that he was very impressed with the 'locking up' bit of my idea, which was encouraging coming from someone so posh. He's so upper-class it's frightening, to tell you the truth.) ④

Eight

As you can imagine, I was totally over the moon, a month later, when Delilah came to summon me to the BOARDROOM! At last! I thought. It'd been a long time in coming, I can tell you. I'd been slaving away, sitting on that stool, year in, year out, for fifteen ruddy years, and now it had arrived: PROMOTION! Or maybe even a SEAT ON THE BOARD!!! In with the new broom - Out with the general public. Oh yes, I was brimming with good ideas for the gallery's future!

Lord Walton

Delilah

Gareth

Absolutely no idea

I found His Lordship very much in the pink. He'd probably been enjoying all his high-life and money and deer-shooting and teas with the toffs at Buckingham Palace because he was extreeeeeeeemly pleased to see me. Actually the whole Board was - and then I found out why. They needed a very, very, important man to go to AMERICA!!! and they couldn't think of anyone more very, very, important than YOURS TRULY. I was so excited I nearly needed the toilet twice.

Nine

Nice teeth

The plane ride was less exciting than I'd hoped. I had a first-class seat next to a first-class STUPID-HEAD. He really was a MR. GRUMPY TROUSERS. Never the less, I did my bit to cheer the flight up for everyone because I'm like that. They enjoyed the little trick I do where I throw an M&M in the air and catch it in my mouth. There's nothing worse than having misery guts' all over the place, is there?

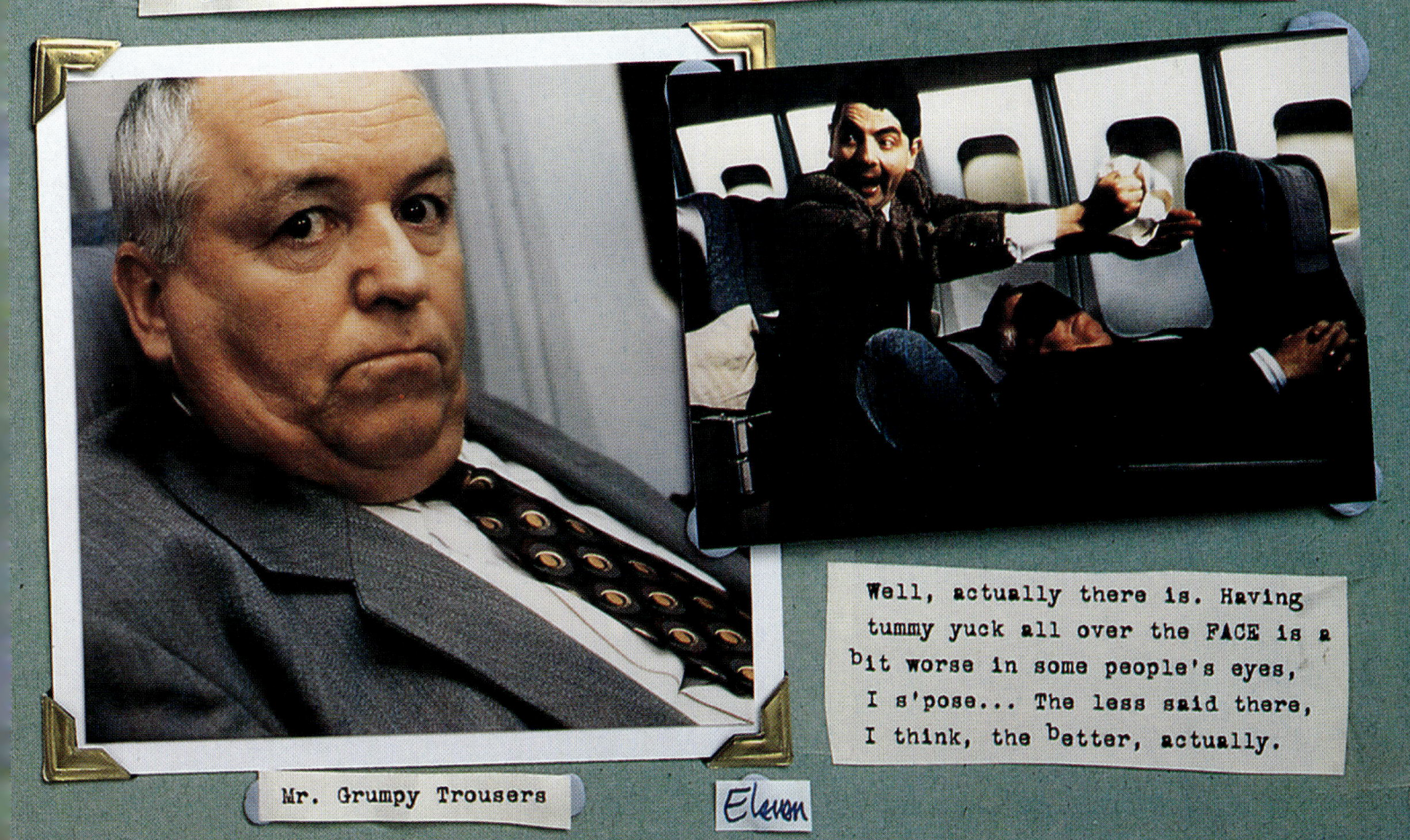

Well, actually there is. Having tummy yuck all over the FACE is a bit worse in some people's eyes, I s'pose... The less said there, I think, the better, actually.

Mr. Grumpy Trousers

Eleven

HEALTH WARNING

IT IS VERY DANGEROUS TO THROW SWEETS INTO THE AIR AND CATCH THEM IN YOUR MOUTH! YOU REALLY MUST NOT TRY IT, UNDERSTAND? YOU COULD CHOKE! BRAINY-HEADS PLEASE EXPLAIN THIS TO ALL STUPID-HEADS IN THE VICINITY, FOR HEAVEN'S SAKE. END OF WARNING.

(Signed Mr. Bean)

On my arrival at Los Angeles Airport I was quite disconcerted to discover that there was a price on my head. I had seen no WANTED posters of me on the plane and was therefore taken aback somewhat on being run to ground by a mean and desperate posse. Well, actually they were just ordinary American cops and had arrested me for illegal possession of an imaginary gun. I don't go anywhere without my imaginary gun and anyway, I couldn't see what all the fuss was about... It only shoots imaginary bullets!

My imaginary Smith & Wesson

Desperate posse

The UGLIEST, and by far the most UNBALANCED, of these STUBBLE-JAWED gun slingers (ordinary American cops) was as bald as a baby's buttock. A sure sign of a STUPID-HEAD in my book and therefore bound to be the Sheriff. ⑦

I was darn-tootin' up the wrong creek. The Sheriff turned out to be an African-looking gentleman who spoke with an American accent and had the hugest shirt, jacket and trousers I think I have ever SEEN! He was an awful, awful, scary man called Brutus.

Whoops!

BRUTUS

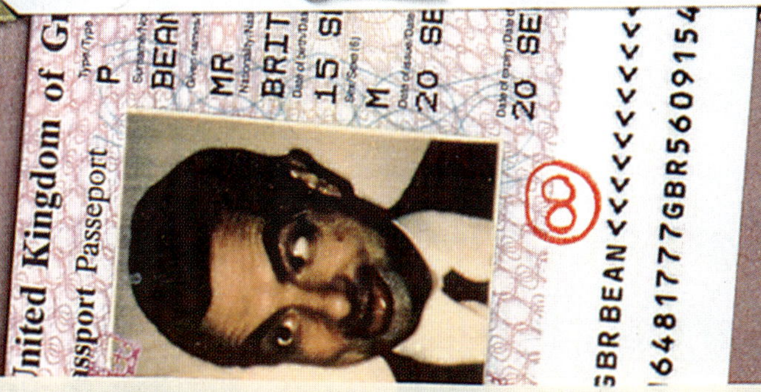

Sheriff Brutus kept me waiting around for a ruddy lifetime and not a cup of tea in sight... And I hadn't even done ANYTHING! Then, eventually, he got one of his STUPID-HEAD deputies to man-handle me into a taxi. (I shall, of course, be writing to President Clinton on that matter. He'll put the stick about, don't YOU worry.) ⑨

⑧

Thirteen

(An excellent poem by Mr. Bean, A.A. R.A.C. T.S.B.)

I like to BE in America.
People say, GEE in America.
They also say, HI in America.
I'll never say, BYE to America.
I like to BE in America.
Bagels for TEA in America.
Scoff like a PIG in America
Till you're stomach's as BIG as AMER- I -CA!

Chorus:
Da da de de de de de da de da da dum...dum...
BURP BURP!
De da da burp! Burp!! De da da burp! Burp!
Bum bum bum bum...! etc.

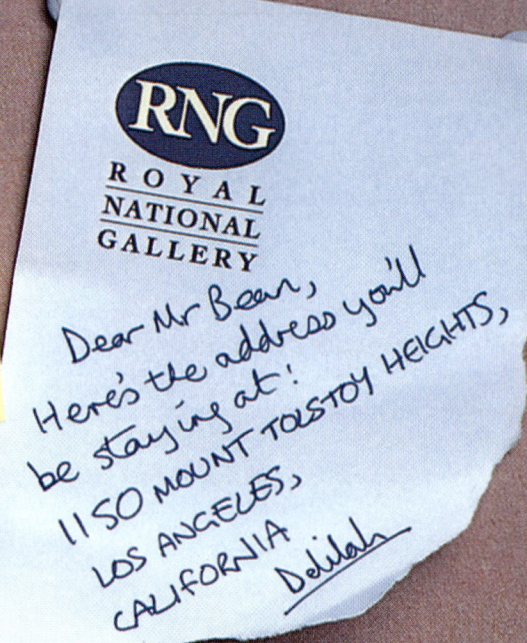

Dear Mr Bean,
Here's the address you'll be staying at:
1150 MOUNT TOLSTOY HEIGHTS,
LOS ANGELES,
CALIFORNIA

Delilah

I had been given an address on a piece of paper by Delilah, at the gallery, before I left home. This turned out to be EXTREEEMLY useful, actually, because when the taxi man asked me if I had an address, I told him, "c/o Mrs. Wicket, 'Daffodils', 12 Arbor Road, Highbury, London N10. England," and he said that another address might be better and did I have one... so I gave him the only other one I had which was the one that Delilah gave me and this taxi man said that that was a bit more phuttin' like it (or somesuch) and dropped me off outside the most appalling looking house on God's earth. ⑩

APPALLING HOUSE

Me (sleeping?!)

← Toothpaste (mint)   Fourteen

It later turned out that, actually, this house was of an extreeeeemly tasteful design, aptly befitting David Langley, curator of an EXTREEEEMLY famous art museum called THE GRIERSON GALLERY. Anyway, on Delilah's piece of paper it said that I was meant to be staying here. I rang the bell but there seemed to be no one at home. "TYPICAL," I thought, "What ruddy manners do you call this?" The spare front door key was under the frog so I let myself in. It's always, always, always, under the most stupid object isn't it? Ask yourself, given the choice of putting your key under a brick or under Kermit the frog, where would you put it...? EXACTLY. Thank you. It's just as well STUPID-HEAD burglars don't know the art of key hiding or we'd all be up the ruddy CREEK. ⑪ Appendix STILL at back ⟶

Frog in question

There really WAS no one in the house (OR SO I THOUGHT AT THE TIME!!!). Not that it mattered though; I was still able to get on with my 'going to bed' routine: Don pajammies, splash face, scrub teeth, De-wax ears, rinse socks, big cough, bed... zzzzzzzzzzzzzzzzzzzzzzz.

Fifteen   More mint

Next morning the family decided to turn up, and in spite of their extraordinary grumpy faces they turned out to be a very nice family indeed. Apparently, they had all dressed up smart and gone to the airport the night before to meet me, and would have succeeded if I hadn't been ambushed by Sheriff Brutus and his posse in the meantime.

My friend, David

The Langleys were not a bad bunch at all – and I could tell that David's wife, Alison, was simply over the moon to have me stay. She just would not stop SMILING AT ME! Which is always a good sign in my book. And the children? Well, there was a lovely family resemblance in them though Jennifer was taller than Kevin, which I put down to age, and she was a lot more female than Kevin which is often the case with people who are practicing to grow up to be women. I wouldn't know.

Alison

Sixteen

If I ever had to be a married man I think the woman would have to be like Alison only a bit taller and fatter with a different nose and shoes. And if I accidentally had a son he would have to be like Kevin but not as clever and nice because it's a parent's job to tell children off all the time and I wouldn't be able to do that with Kevin because he's too good. My Landlady, Mrs. Wicket, absolutely bawls HER son, Ernest, into the ground. The whole street hears it. Ernest Wicket is always sobbing in the hall cupboard and he's THIRTY TWO so everyone knows that Mrs. Wicket must be one HELL of a mother. No, my little boy would have to be the naughtiest boy in the world so everyone could hear me rant and rave and yell and scream at him like Mrs. Wicket and know that I was a good dad. Actually, I think I would be a good dad anyway because I can throw sweets into the air and catch them in my mouth. I showed Kevin how to do it and he was VERY impressed indeeeeeed. There's another good trick I do with sticking bus tickets to my eyelids and blinking fast. I didn't show Kevin that one because I'm saving it up in case I have to have a little boy of my own one day.

12

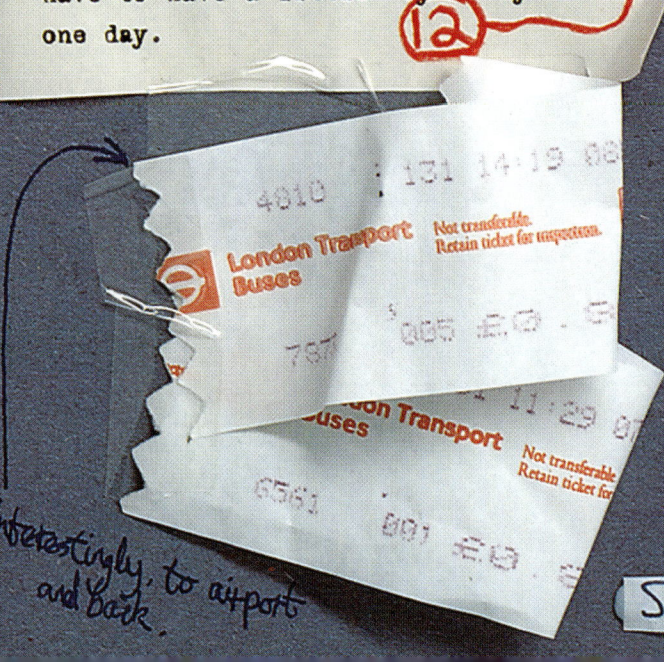

Interestingly, to airport and back.

Kevin

And as for Jennifer; talk about MISS RUDDY GRUMPY TROUSERS!

Seventeen

By the way, it's interesting isn't it, that wherever you go in the world, foreigners all have their funny little ways of saying, "Mr." For instance, in France, they'd call me: "Miss you, Bean", which is quite endearing. In Germany it would be "Hairy, Bean." Mmmm, there you go. In Spain: "Seen yours, Bean", which is alarming, frankly - and in America, it transpires, I was to be called: "Doctor, Bean." That's what David kept calling me anyway, which was confusing TO SAY THE LEAST! because a doctor is quite an important person where I come from (England). There again, the label had a BRILLIANT professional ring to it, and, after all, the Royal National Gallery had sent me here because I was VERY, VERY, IMPORTANT! So in the end I found "Doctor" quite a fitting title for me, actually.

The Gallery

The Gallery again

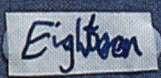

The gallery where David worked was an absolute SIGHT, I can tell you. It looked like someone had blown it up with dynamite and stuck it back together ALL WRONG. I wondered if God had created it on the same day as David's house... and horse poo and the word: 'FART'. Then, I was duly surprised and humbled on being informed that this, as with David's abode, was an EXTREEEEMLY tasteful building designed by a Japanese gentleman who's name sounded like a brand of soap powder. Keep taking the tablets, Mr. Sud Soo, that's my advice - and GET BACK TO THE DRAWING BOARD!!!

Ruddy water!

Lovely fan

True to form, I had one of my usual embarrassing troubles in the loo before I had to meet the VEEEEERY IMPORTANT people who ran the gallery. Luckily no one noticed the sopping wet map of India on the front my trousers when I entered the boardroom. That's because there's an art to dealing with these nasty little setbacks and I'm a MASTER of it - have to be. This is another example of the Universe being made up of STUPID-HEADS and BRAINY-HEADS. Some STUPID-HEAD did the plumbing in the toilet all wrong so my flies got splashed by a tap, while, somewhere else, a clever BRAINY-HEAD, invented the electric fan which is perfect for drying one's map of India. Thankfully, there's a method in the Almighty's madness. I mean, has it not struck you that if God hadn't invented the 'ear' and the 'plug' on the same day we would have nothing to shut out people's STUPID YAPPING? It's certainly crossed my mind once or twice, and, cleverly, these objects have a job independently of one another. That's the marvel.

Map of India

Nineteen

Once the laws of science had rallied and restored my dignity in the trouser department I was able to concentrate a little on the VERY IMPORTANT MEETING in hand. It was about all sorts of interesting things, from what I could gather, and someone's mother was coming home after being away for a hundred and fifty years. How nice. I nearly mentioned that she would most definitely be a SKELETON by now - but decided not to rock the boat. I'd only been in America for twelve hours and had yet to gauge exactly how STUPID these people were. Besides, it might have been DAVID's mother they were talking about. No point in being rude. Not yet. There was plenty of time for that later. Everyone was being so nice to me - calling me "Doctor" this and "Doctor" that. Didn't want to spoil it all, really.

13

Mr. Grierson, David's very serious boss.
A VERY IMPORTANT MAN

Bernice. Who's job was an absolute mystery to me but seemed quite IMPORTANT INDEED.

Walter. STUPID-HEAD.
Not the least bit important at all.

Twenty

Welcome Home, Mom!

America's most famous portrait returns after 150 years

By Poppy Alcock
Art Correspondent

Whistler's Mother, which has always been regarded as America's most famous painting, is coming home, it was announced yesterday. The portrait has been acquired from the Musée d'Orsay in Paris by the Grierson Gallery in California thanks to generous benefactor General Newton who paid fifty million dollars to have the painting restored to its home country.

Comte Garcon de Bon, curator of the Musée d'Orsay described the sale of the painting as: "A great loss to France," but added "I will soon be resigning my position here at the gallery."

The return of the painting was announced by George Grierson himself at a brief press conference at the Gallery. "From now on," he said, "*Whistler's Mother* will live right here in L.A. where she belongs."

On questioning General Newton, it emerged that he is planning to use the painting as a centerpiece for his collection of World War II despatch motorcycles. "They need a focal point and *Whistler's Mother* is it," he said.

The painting will be unveiled at a special ceremony at the Gallery in a few weeks time.

→ *Americans can't SPELL! Tsk! Tsk!*

General Newton, top, and Whistler's Mother, *bought for $50 million.*

What the...?

Dear, oh dear, oh dear

BONKERS!

ZZZZZZZZZZZZZZZZZZZZ...

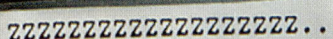

The paintings in the Grierson Gallery were just as interesting as the ones where I work in England which was excellent.

When David took me back to his house Alison suddenly went on holiday with the children – which was a charming, off-the-cuff idea, I thought. I don't think she had even told David that she was going because he was just as knocked for six as I was. A nice break in the mountains with her mother. SMASHING. Talking of 'SMASHING' I did a bit of that to David and Alison's honeymoon photograph seconds before Alison had her holiday idea. Luckily it was an awful, soppy, slushy, blubbery, YUCK, YUCK, YUCKY, picture with a dog in it that no one would have had on their wall in ten million years. So off they all went leaving me and my new friend to have our own fun for the weekend.

YUCK!

Alone at last

Twenty Two (I wish I'd done 1, 2, 3 etc I am soooo boooored of numbering buddy pages like this)

CLICK!

'ME AND DAVID "DO" L..A'
(An exceptionally good poem by Mr. Bean).

With DAVID'S family
out of the way
David and I could
have fun in L.A.
We got in his car
and HE TOOK ME SOMEwhere
WHERE ALL OF THE WOMEN
HAD BIG STUPID hair.
THE MEN ALL HAD WIGS
AND GREAT hairy CHESTS,
which THEY COULD HARDLY CONTAIN
IN THEIR BLACK RUBBER VESTS.
THEN, Some were so old
their skin hung in ripples
And the rest were tattooed
with rings through their nipples...

"Cheese!"

SNAP!

(But I digress...)

HANG ON ONE RUDDY MINUTE......!!!
.... But But but but but but but but but but but but but but but but but
but but but but but but but but but but WHAT THE? but b but but but but but but OH
MY GOD!!! but but but but but but but but but but but but but but but but but b b b
but but but but but but YIKES!!! but but but but but but but but b b b b b b b b b
b b b b b b b b b b b b b b b b b b b b b b b b b b b b b b b b b b I
B B B B B B B B B B B B B B B B B b b b b b b b b b b b b b b b b
DON'T RUDDY BELIEVE IT...! B B B B b b b b b b b b b b b b b b b b B B B B B B
b b b b b b b b b b b b b b b b b OH LORDY LORDY HEAVENS ABOVE! B B B B B B
B B B B B B B B B B B B B B B B B B B B B B B B B B B B B B B B B B
b b b b b b b b b b b b b AAAAHHHHRRRRGGGG!!!! b b b b b b
b b b b b b b b b b b b b b b b b b b b b b b b b b b b b b b b B
b B B B B B B B B B B B BB B B B B B B B B B B B B B B B B B B B B
B B B B B B B B B B B B B B B B B B B B B B B BUT THIS IS SIMPLY
AWFUL!!! b b b b b b b b b b b b b b b b b b b b b B B B B B B B B
B B B B B B b b b b b b b b b b b b b b b b b b b b b b b b b b b
b b b B b b b b b b b b b b B B B B B B B B B B B B B B B b b ENOUGH!
ENOUGH!!! b b b B B B B B B B B B B B B B B B B B B B B B B B B B B B
b b b b B B B B B B b b b b b b b b b b b b b b b b b b B
B b b b b b b b b b b b b b b b b b b b b b b b b b b b b
MY Bs ARE BOUNCING ABOUT ALL OVER THE BLINKING SHOP! IT'S SOOOOOOOOOOOOOOOOO BARMY!

Twenty Five

The **BRAINY-HEADS** that you are, I trust you've noticed there are no more bouncing 'b's all over the ruddy place! That's because my **STUPID TYPEWRITER** is at the menders and Mrs. Wicket's **DAFT** son, Ernest, has loaned me this very, very, **MARVELLOUS** computer ditty called a **WORD POSSESSOR**. It possesses all the words you could ever possibly want. It's an absolute **GOD-SEND**, I can tell you (if you've got that sort of money to throw around, obviously. Ernest Wicket can afford it because he stays indoors quite a bit).

...So, anyway, at the end of our lovely day of fun in Los Angeles, I ended up back in trouble with that **STUPID, STUPID, Sheriff Brutus!** What an absolute ruddy inconvenience!

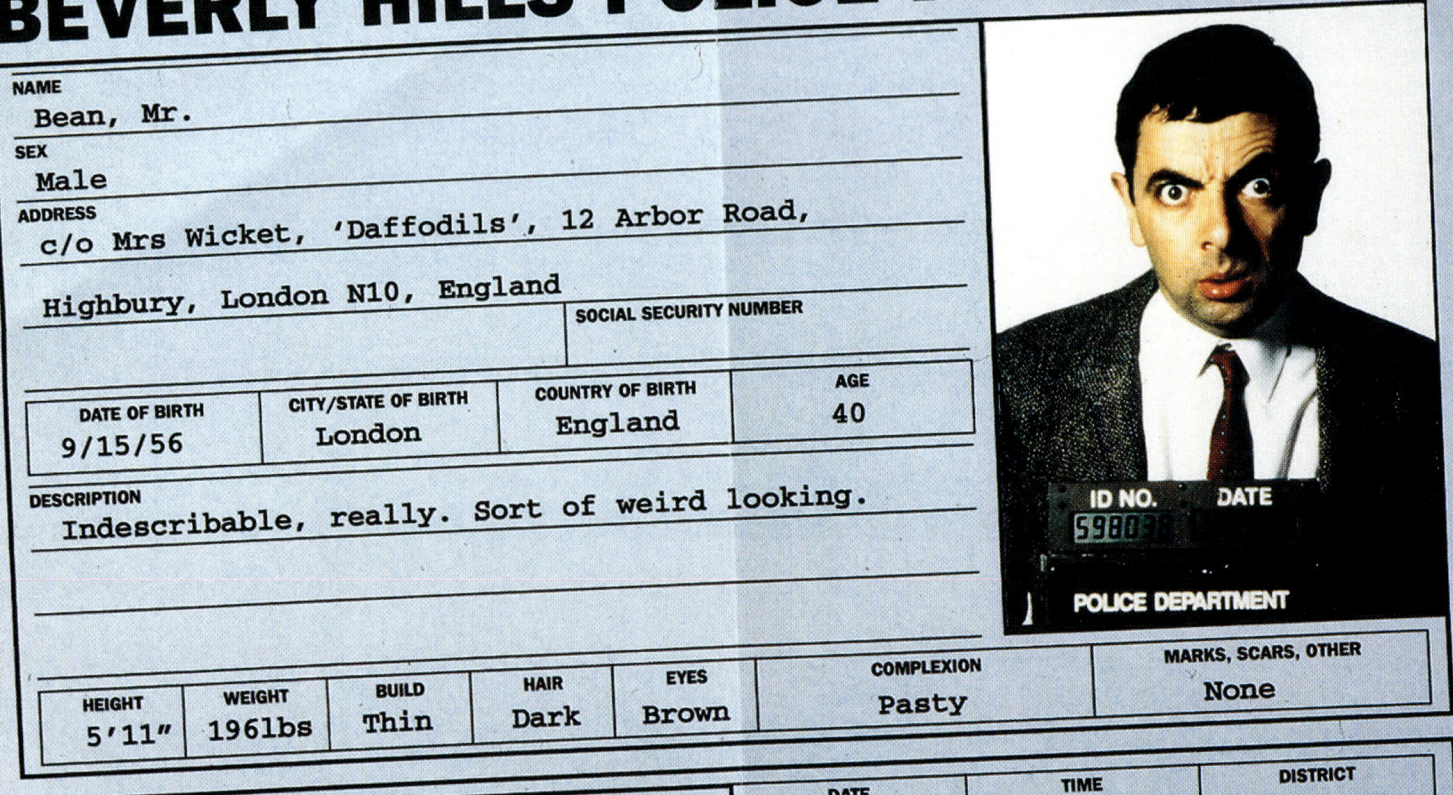

BEVERLY HILLS POLICE DEPARTMENT

NAME: Bean, Mr.
SEX: Male
ADDRESS: c/o Mrs Wicket, 'Daffodils', 12 Arbor Road, Highbury, London N10, England
SOCIAL SECURITY NUMBER:
DATE OF BIRTH: 9/15/56
CITY/STATE OF BIRTH: London
COUNTRY OF BIRTH: England
AGE: 40
DESCRIPTION: Indescribable, really. Sort of weird looking.
ID NO.: 59809
DATE:

HEIGHT: 5'11"
WEIGHT: 196lbs
BUILD: Thin
HAIR: Dark
EYES: Brown
COMPLEXION: Pasty
MARKS, SCARS, OTHER: None

ARREST/INVESTIGATION REPORT

DATE:
TIME: 12.50pm
DISTRICT: Santa Monica

ARRESTING/INVESTIGATING OFFICERS: Captain Irvin Brutus / Detective Bob Baker
INCIDENT LOCATION: The Ride of Doom, Santa Monica Pier, Santa Monica, L.A.
ARREST/INCIDENT REPORT: My partner and I responded to a radio call requesting assistance at the above locale. On arrival we found several citizens limping along with broken legs and arms. Apparently the ride had gone crazy and injured these folks. I then spotted the English guy and recognised him to be Mr. Bean. I had interviewed him before on a suspected arms charge. Detective Baker and myself brought him in where he admitted sabotage.

Twenty Six

Who is that intelligent looking man?

Ooooh, it's me!

BRUTUS!

He was just as AWFUL as he was the last time our paths crossed - you know, REALLY GRUMPY - Only this time he left me in a room all on my own for hours and hours and hours. It was sooooooooo booooooooring I nearly died (of boredom). Speaking of which, how about a change of tight face...?

14

Twenty Seven

'THE FAT STUPID CAT SPAT ON THE STINKY MAT.'
OH YES, THIS IS MORE LIKE IT... THIS IS WHAT WE
WORD POSSESSOR PEOPLE CALL 'A NEW TIGHT
FACE' AND YOU CAN ALSO DO:

and this and this and this!

Typewriter - eat your heart out!

WORD POSSESSORS RULE, OK!

There really are so many tight FACES TO choose from...!

Twenty Eight

...Anyway, the reason Sheriff Brutus wanted my guts for garters was because I did one of my little 'INTERFERENCES' at a funfair.

You see, there was this thing called: "THE RIDE OF DOOM" and the sign promised it would be: "FRIGHTENING!" But when David and I had a go it was so pansy I didn't even wet my pants once! So I had a little 'INTERFERENCE' with my screwdriver in the control room and Bob's yer Uncle : HELL ON EARTH! Three fractured collarbones, six broken legs, eight dislocated shoulders, a torn hamstring and twelve concussions later (all to other people, fortunately) I was back up in front of Sheriff Brutus. He gave me a right good dressing down, I can tell you, about considering other people and everything - and I must say, in between the pleading and the begging, a lot of what he said made some sense - so I gave it some thought and scoured my inner being for some vestige of remorse - some glimmer of repentance - and eventually realized that my little naughtiness had been worth every ruddy minute! MY 'Ride of Doom' had been exceedingly SUPERB thank you very much.

15

Twenty Nine

What Sheriff, Grumpy Old Trousers Brutus had obviously failed to grasp was that I was A VERY, VERY, IMPORTANT MAN, sent all the way from England because I was so incredibly, incredibly, IMPORTANT. This is another annoying episode that I will have to bring to the attention of President Clinton. Oh yes.

Our Leader.

Sometimes, in my more depressed moments, I imagine that I come from another planet where I am the leader. On my planet we would do things very differently, I can tell you. On my planet everyone would applaud every time I walked into a room. Everywhere I went I would be given free sweets and presents of food (dumplings mainly) and people would queue up to shake my hand. On my planet Sheriff Brutus would be Father Christmas and so would have to be nice to people - which would keep him quite busy, actually, because on my planet it would be Christmas EVERY DAY! Enough of that or I'll... well... just enough of that.

Thirty

Mr. and Mrs. Grierson

That night, after being freed from gaol, David's boss, Mr. Grierson, caught us on the hop when he and his wife suddenly popped round for dinner - and so I had to stuff a turkey, double quick. (Ruddy thing!)

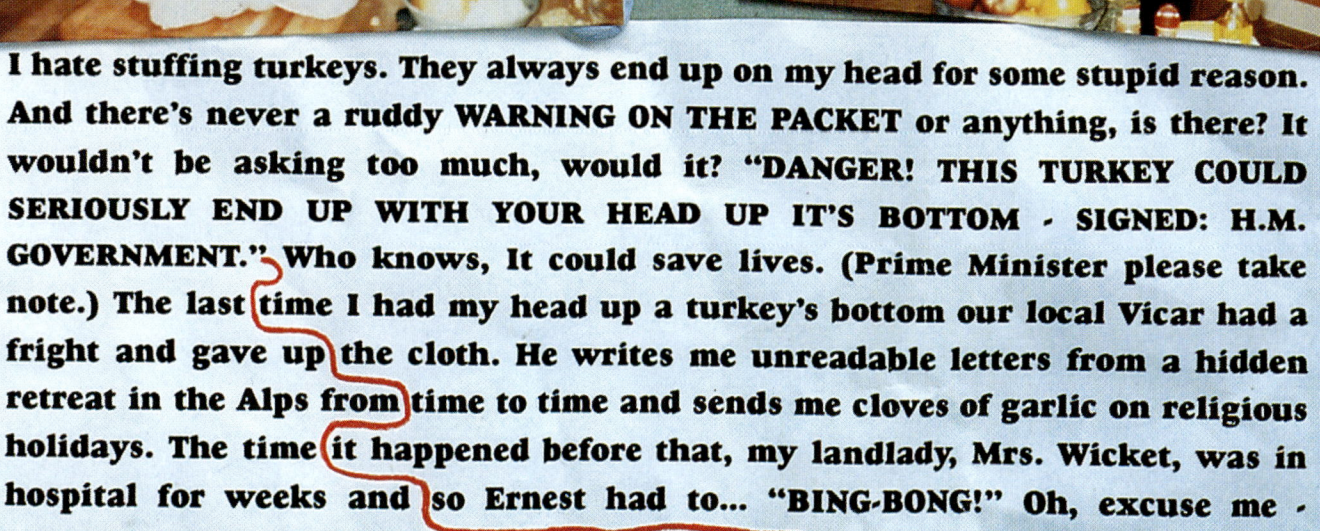

I hate stuffing turkeys. They always end up on my head for some stupid reason. And there's never a ruddy WARNING ON THE PACKET or anything, is there? It wouldn't be asking too much, would it? "DANGER! THIS TURKEY COULD SERIOUSLY END UP WITH YOUR HEAD UP IT'S BOTTOM - SIGNED: H.M. GOVERNMENT." Who knows, It could save lives. (Prime Minister please take note.) The last time I had my head up a turkey's bottom our local Vicar had a fright and gave up the cloth. He writes me unreadable letters from a hidden retreat in the Alps from time to time and sends me cloves of garlic on religious holidays. The time it happened before that, my landlady, Mrs. Wicket, was in hospital for weeks and so Ernest had to... "BING-BONG!" Oh, excuse me - someone at the door. . . . .

Thirty One

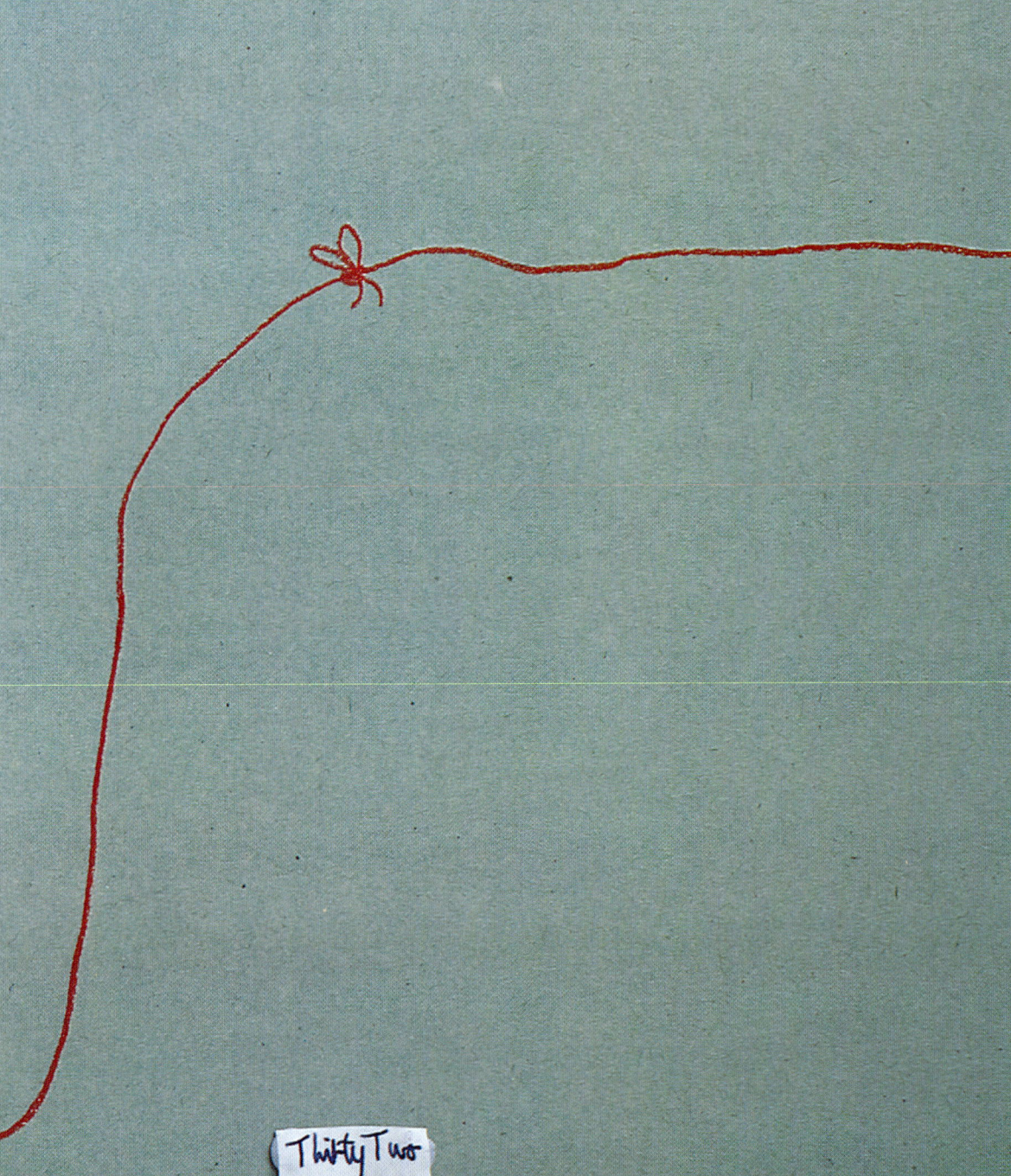

Thirty Two

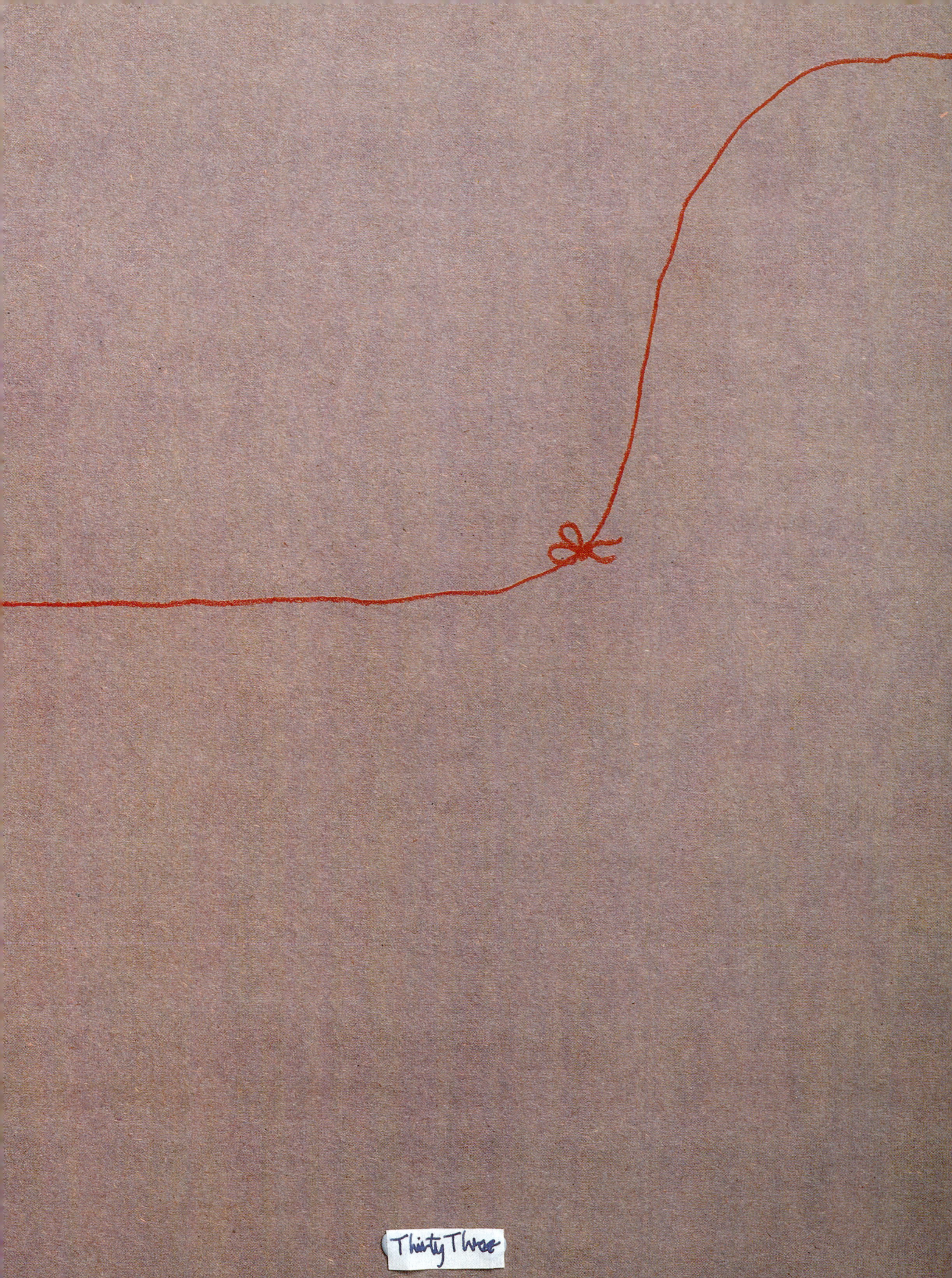

.....Sorry about that. It was Ernest Wicket, popped up to take back his word possessor. He said he needs it to write his novel - which would be a bit difficult actually, Ernest, because you are a RUDDY GREAT STUPID-HEAD! You wouldn't know a novel if it wore a huge pink hat and danced a jig with no clothes on! I WAS REALLY ENJOYING USING THAT WORD POSSESSOR!!! I feel SOOOOOOOO ANGREEEEEE...! Deep breath... deep breath... Ernest is jealous about this book because it WILL be a RAVING SUCCESS!!! HATE! HATE! HATE! HATE! HATE...! Deep breath... ahhhhhhh... ahhhhhhh... ahhhhhhh... ....that's better... ah yes.

Fear not, gentle reader. As you can see, I've been down to the typewriter shop: B B B B b b b b bub bub bub bub bbbbb BBBBB... That's b-b-b-etter. Every b is beautifully back in obeyance - and this lovely old typewriter is like brand spanking new - now that it's been mended. (18)

David slightly mad, I think

After the turkey had been jammed in the microwave for twenty minutes, had exploded, and we had sent the Griersons home hungry David decided to ask me a few 'casual' questions over an interesting snack - i.e. a packet of frozen peas. I record that conversation here VERBATIM on the off-chance it may help psychiatrists if David ends up in the LOONY BIN one day - because I must say; his manner that night took an odd turn which had me fearing for his SANITY. See what YOU make of it, for Heaven's sake!

Thirty Four

DAVID: Bean, I think we are going to have to be honest with each other. I can't deny that over the last days some suspicions have started to gather in my mind. Can I ask you a few direct questions?

I nod.

DAVID: First. Are you a Doctor?

I shake my head. I can see him getting slowly het-up. Not my ruddy fault - It's not ME that's been calling me Doctor!

DAVID: Do you actually, in fact, work at the Royal National Gallery?

I nod. Why not? It was the truth.

DAVID: Well, that's something. But... do you know anything about art?

That question had me somewhat stumped if I'm truthful - where was all this leading to though I wondered?

DAVID: For example... was Leonardo da Vinci an American basketball player?

The name meant nothing to me, of course, but David was desperate for the right answer. He was very tense and there were strange red shadows in his eyes like... like there was some grizzly animal in his skull using his eyes as windows. I tried to act natural and gave the answer I thought might best please him:

ME: Yes.

This is where I thought David had gone STARK RAVING MAD because when I gave that answer he hid his face in his hands, almost as if he were trying to hide from me the windows of his eyes. His shoulders jerked up and down - and he wasn't laughing either - It was a SURE sign there was madness afoot, in my book. As you can appreciate, it was a very odd episode indeed - one which still puzzles me from time to time... no less for what happened next, because at that precise moment, David's family popped in to see how we were getting on. It was a short stay. About four seconds, then they headed for the hills again.

I wonder if they had seen, as I had that night, the BEAST in David Langley. But I digress.

Thirty Five

Next day, at the gallery, I realized what an absolute twit I'd been! Now it all made sense! At that first VERY IMPORTANT meeting when the VERY IMPORTANT people at the gallery were talking about someone's mother coming home after a hundred and fifty years they were talking about a VERY, VERY, VERY, IMPORTANT PAINTING which was painted by the VERY, VERY, VERY, IMPORTANT bloke who painted it. Interestingly, that VERY, VERY, VERY, IMPORTANT bloke was the son of the old woman in the VERY, VERY, VERY, IMPORTANT painting which this VERY IMPORTANT bloke had painted. And that bloke's name was WHISTLER. (Dead now but apparently quite a big knob in his day (YAWN). Which all meant that this painting was the most IMPORTANT painting in the world. Which I could seriously believe given all the FUSS.

Mrs. Whistler
on the wall
Sitting down
you look so tall.
Standing up,
your dress might fall
And flash your
under-where-withal.

Thirty Six

Elmer

Frankly I couldn't see what all the fuss was about. Mrs. Whistler looked like any grumpy old biddy who'd just had her telly taken away to stop her spitting at it or something. (YAWN) It did strike me that the frame might fetch a couple of bob in a posh junk shop, though. Whatever. Anyway. Everyone was congratulating my friend, David, because, apparently, it was his idea to bring the old bird home to roost in the first place. Elmer, the head of SECURITY, gave David the very special SECURITY key card that opened the high SECURITY burglar-proof SECURITY case that kept the painting SECURE. Good thinking, I thought. Then they all went off with Elmer, the head of SECURITY, to look at the new high SECURITY system, system, gizmo system SECURITY wassit and everything (YAWN AGAIN) and left me alone with Mrs. Whistler.

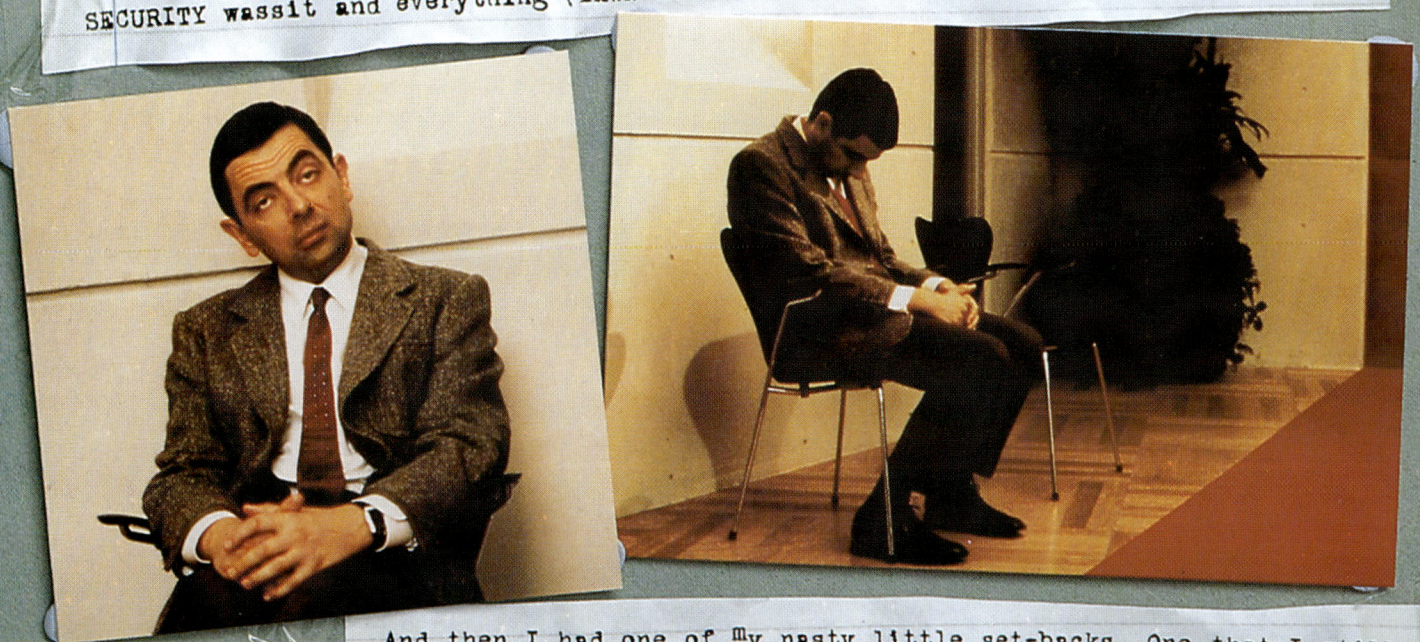

And then I had one of my nasty little set-backs. One that I still re-live at least three times a day. It goes something like this:

Thirty Seven

I SNEEZE AND AN UNMENTIONABLE GLOBULE LEAVES MY NOSE AT A HUNDRED MILES AN HOUR AND HITS MRS. WHISTLER, SQUARE IN THE FACE... AAARRRGGGHHH... QUICK, HANKIE! HANKIE! WIPE IT OFF WITH HANKIE. YES. YES. YES. NO. NO. OH NOOOOOOOOO... INK! INK! INK! INK! BLUE INK ON THE HANKIE FROM A LEAKY RUDDY FOUNTAIN PEN! ALL OVER HER F...F...F...FACE... WHY? OH WHY? OH WHY...? OH WHY? OH WHY? DEATH COME QUICK! WRAP ME IN YOUR WARM DARK NIGHT...! WATER! WATER! WATER! YES, YES, WATER! AH HA! A VASE OF FLOWERS! WATER TO THE RESCUE... OH SWEET RELIEF. NO WATER! NO WATER! NO RUDDY WATER IN THE **@&%$* VASE BECAUSE THEY ARE DRIED **@&%$* FLOWERS! DEATH, TAKE ME TO A PLACE OF REST AND... CALM... CALM... PANIC! PANIC! PANIC! PANIC! PANIC! NO WATER, WATER. SPIT? SPIT, SPIT, SPIT... CAN'T REACH THE PAINTING. TAKE IT DOWN AND SPIT ON MY SHIRT AND CLEAN OFF THE INK AND OH NOOOOOOOO...! STAMP, STAMP, STAMP, BIG FEET, FEET, FEET. ALL OVER MRS. WHISTLER... GETAWAY... GET AWAY... GET WATER.... RUN. FIND WATER... AH HA, MEN'S ROOM. GOOD GOOD. WATER IN THE TOILET. GOOD. GOOD. THANK YOU GOD... TOILET BRUSH. SCRUB, SCRUB, SCRUB... KNOCK, KNOCK, KNOCK, AT THE RUDDY DOOR.

Thirty Eight

MAN IN CORRIDOR NEEDS TO WEE, WEE, WEE, WEE, OH ME, ME, ME... OH HEEEELP MEEEEEEE... CALM... CALM... CALM.... CUNNING PLAN! CUNNING PLAN! WHERE IS CUNNING PLAN??? HERE IT COMES... HERE IT COMES... PUT PAINTING OUT OF WINDOW? GOOD IDEA! HOORAY! MAN HAS WEE. HE NO SEE... GOOD. GOOD. ME IN STOREROOM NEXT-DOOR NOW - GOOD. GOOD. GOOD CUNNING PLAN... GET OUT OF WINDOW WHERE MRS. WHISTLER SITS ON THE LEDGE AND TAKES IN THE VIEW, FOUR FLOORS UP, ON A LEDGE OUTSIDE LOO... WHOA! IT'S A B-B-B-BIT HIGH UP... GET PAINTING... GET... GOT IT! BACK IN THE STOREROOM... OH GLORY... WHAT'S THIS? SPECIAL STINKY STUFF IN A RUSTY TIN TO CLEAN OFF STAINS? YEEEEEEES!!!!! CLEAN, CLEAN, CLEAN AND HOPE, HOPE, HOPE... YES, YES, YES, NO MORE INK STAIN. NO MORE, NO MORE. ALL GONE!!! EUREKA!!! ALL GONE. LUMMY, LUMMY. CALM, CALM, CALM... NORMAL, NORMAL, NORMAL! MUST TAKE THE PAINTING BACK NOW - TO THE... AAAAAAARRRRRRRGGGGGGGHHHHHHH...!!!!!!! MRS. WHISTLER'S FACE GOES BUBBLE, BUBBLE, WRITHE AND GURGLE, FROTH AND GUNGE AND YUCK...! RUB AND RUB AND RUB AND ALL GONE... ALL GONE... FACE ALL GONE AWAY... ALL GONE... BARE CANVAS... NO HOPE... NO FACE... ONLY PAIN... ALL GONE... ONLY PAIN... AHHHHHHH... CALM... CALM.... ONLY PAIN...

Thirty Nine

Planet Bean

PLUTO · JUPITER · EARTH · MARS · NEPTUNE · URANUS · SATURN · MERCURY · VENUS · SUN

On my planet there would be no paintings. There would be things that LOOKED like paintings but you couldn't sneeze on them or anything and they wouldn't go bubble, bubble, writhe and gurgle, froth and yuck when you put special stinky stuff from rusty tins on them. They would be made of the most indestructible matter in the universe and be locked up in a magic cavern a thousand miles underground with super-duper force-fields around them guarded by killer fairies. And people wouldn't be allowed to go near them and if they did, and they sneezed on them by accident, the killer fairies would atomize them with ray-guns - except, of course, if it was me that sneezed on them - then they would just say, "It's okay, it's only nice Mr. Bean, the leader of our planet. We won't tell anybody that you've destroyed the most important painting in the World. Here, oh Leader, have a lovely cup of tea and a biscuit. Perhaps a peaceful lie down before you have to go back up and face your adoring public." That's how it would all be on My planet.

Forty

David was very understanding about my little setback under the circumstances. The BEAST in him broke loose but didn't lay a finger on me, which was excellent. Instead, David ranted and raved with blood-shot eyes for a few minutes then suggested that we found a bar and got totally drunk.

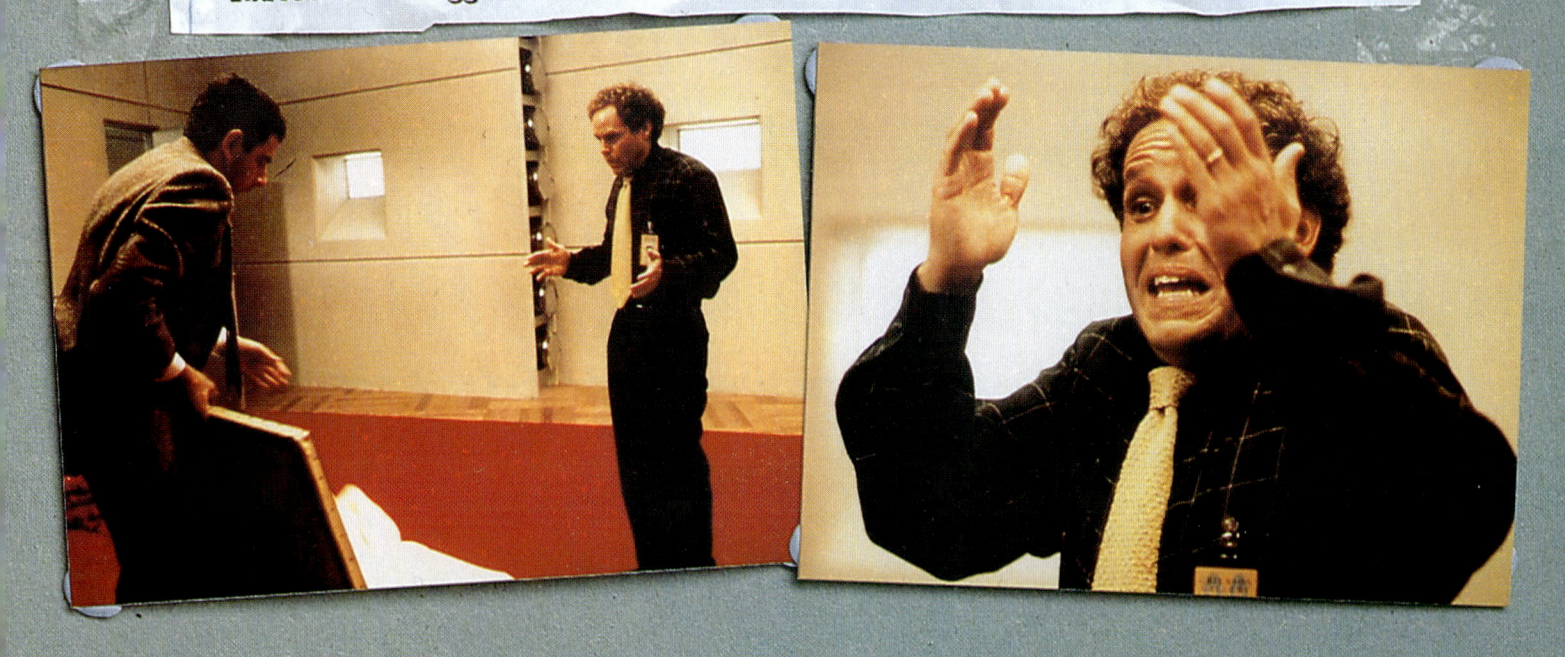

I had done what I could under the circumstances. (20)

Forty One

I think what worried my friend, David, most was what other people – particularly his BOSS – were going to do about the destruction of Whistler's Mother – and, given that David was responsible for her, how long he would have to SPEND IN PRISON. A tricky one. I wouldn't have liked to have been in his shoes, I can tell you. After downing six or seven rather pretty drinks with fruit and umbrellas in them it could have been Christmas for all I knew. And the booze certainly made David forget that he was going to die in prison, probably. Ho hum.

A CAUTIONARY MESSAGE FROM YOUR AUTHOR!
I cannot state the following more strongly: I certainly do NOT condone getting drunk to anyone. I suspect it's the sort of thing STUPID-HEADS do to make themselves more STUPID. I therefore declare that this, my FIRST drunken binge, being a shameful and regrettable episode, will certainly be my LAST drunken binge, and one that I shall regret for the rest of my life - (if I can, by some miracle, ever remember any of it. Thank you.)
END OF CAUTIONARY MESSAGE FROM YOUR AUTHOR!

Forty Two

From what I can remember, Alison was at home when we stumbled in... Yes she was... that's right, because she was in a blazing mood and gave me and David a right dressing down, I can tell you. She and the children had come home from the hills so that they could all be a family again - which was nice - but now seeing David as drunk as a toff she made up her mind to leave him for ever and ever and ever - Which was NOT nice - and we both had to sleep on the couch that night which was even WORSE in my book. It took me absolute eons to get to sleep and once I DID manage to accomplish something nearing slumber I had RUDDY GREAT NIGHTMARES for crying out loud!

'MY REOCCURRING NIGHTMARE'

Alison, dressed as Mrs. Whistler, shuffled into the room, went out again, came in again, went out again, came in again, went out again, came in again, went out again. That was my reoccurring nightmare. The next one was EVEN WORSE!

'THE EVEN WORSE NEXT ONE'

Mrs. Whistler, shuffled into the room and said, "I've been sitting down for a hundred and fifty years now and me bum's as numb as Mrs. Wicket's poorly leg. Ooooooooo, and I could MURDER a cup of tea." David, who was at that moment disguised as a CUP OF TEA, rattled nervously in his saucer. He was, alas, far too slow for Alison (for it was really SHE in the Mrs. Whistler disguise) who brought a refrigerator down on him from a great hight, having effortlessly plucked it from the corner of the kitchen with her thirty-foot-long lizard tongue. David went to pieces (literally), sending shards of bone china all over the RUDDY SHOP! One of the larger pieces knocked over a rusty tin on a high shelf and all this stinky stuff poured out and went bubble, bubble, writhe and gurgle, froth and yuck all over Alison who turned to ashes... and then I woke up!

Forty Three

WHAT MY DREAM MEANS

1.) Cup of tea = David/all things nice.
2.) Stinky bubble yuck stuff = Doom/Hell/the enemy/WEll!
3.) Whistler's Mother = My dirty deed incarnate.
4.) Alison = Voice of reason.
5.) Refrigerator = Bosom of the family.
6.) Alison's lizard tongue = Lifeline/rescue/hope.
7.) Mrs. Wicket's Poorly leg = Heck knows.
8.) Kevin = Society part 1./Shortness.
9.) Jennifer = Anarchy/chaos.
10.) Mucky fingerprint = Mucky fingerprint.

Forty Four

Meanings, meanings, meanings... Over a troubled midnight snack in the Langley kitchen, I wracked my brain for a meaning to my VERY, VERY, FRIGHTENING DREAMS. Then I remembered something David had slurred at me back in that bar earlier:

"What happened here, Beany? We asked the Royal National Gallery of England to send us their top art expert. They send us the guy from Texas Chainsaw Massacre. You moved into my house, my wife has left me. She might have done it anyway - but you were the ten ton weight with the stupid haircut that broke the camel's back. It would have been better if I'd never been born... (echo:) never been born... never been born... never been born..."

Yes, maybe David WAS a tad upset about something but I couldn't for the life of me....THEN THE PENNY TWIGGED! David's problem was MEEEEEEEE!!!!! Of course...! The deep, inner meaning, of my nightmare became as crystal! It was MEEEEEEEEE!!!!!

Forty Five

TIME FOR ACTION!

Forty Six

SEE HOW IT ALL SUDDENLY MADE SENSE? NOT A PRETTY PICTURE - BUT ONE THAT I HAD CREATED. MY DREAM HAD MIRRORED THE AWFUL REALITY OF IT ALL. I HAD DESTROYED NOT ONLY A PRICELESS WORK OF ART BUT ALSO A MAN, HIS CAREER, AND HIS LOVELY FAMILY. NOW IT WAS UP TO ME TO TURN BACK THE CLOCK AND MAKE EVERYTHING BETTER AGAIN! IT WAS TIME TO BREAK INTO THE GRIERSON GALLERY! IT WAS TIME FOR ACTION!

GRIERSON GALLERY
GG

'TOOLS FOR THE JOB'

- 1 Black woolly hat.
- 1 Black woolly jumper.
- 6 Eggs.
- 1 Pair of rubber gloves.
- 1 Skateboard.
- 1 Crocodile oven-glove.
- 1 Cooking basin
- 1 Whisk.
- David's Security key-card.
- 15 Sticks of chewing-gum.
- 1 Pizza-cutter.
- 1 Zebra oven-glove.
- 2 Bottles of nail varnish.
- 1 Car jack.
- 1 Hair-drier.
- 1 Paintbrush.
- 1,000,000 tons of RUDDY GOOD LUCK!

Forty Seven

Forty Eight

MISSION ACCOMPLISHED - ON MY WAY HOME!

Coincidentally, it is also ti^{m}e for ^{m}e to break into Ernest Wicket's roo^m downstairs and use his WORD POSSESSOR! These ju^{m}ping '^{m}'s are driving ^{m}e up the ruddy wall and round the spout! Don't think I hadn't noticed the ruddy things ^{m}eandering ^{m}alignantly all over ^{m}y ruddy pages earlier cos I had! I just didn't want to interrupt ^{m}y very I^{M}PORTANT creative flow, that's all.

Forty Nine

Ah ha! This is more ruddy like it for blinking hell's bells!

👉

No... but **seriously**... (TEE HEE HEE...) I dooooooo love this modern machine! Shhhhh... Ernest Wicket is out **(of his mind, actually)** at night school and so I have broken in through his toilet window and found his word possessor on the kitchen table - Yipppeee!

Interestingly, he has left some pages of his so-called novel around the place for burglars to read. I have read some of it and as I expected; **IT IS COMPLETE AND UTTER RUBBISH!!!** (I have written helpful notes all over it to that effect!) ㉓

Anyway, where were we? Oh yes... the morning, after my brilliant James Bond clever wassit at the gallery, I did my best to act natural. It was funny because David was being a real scaredy-cat about everyone finding out about the destroyed Mrs. Whistler, tee hee hee...

...and grumpy old Jennifer didn't do much for David's scaredy-cat mood either because she went off to school on the back of an HORRENDOUSLY DANGEROUS motorbike driven by what seemed to be a rather interesting breed of dog.

Fifty One

Jennifer and Stingo

General Newton

Me with General Newton taken by me

Of course, David was even more scaredy-cat when we got to the gallery. Today was to be the grand unveiling of Whistler's Mother and General Newton had come to do the honours. This General bloke was the most IMPORTANT man in America, apparently, because it was he that had stumped-up the $50,000,000 to buy the Whistler painting for the Grierson Gallery in the first place.

Fifty Two

$50,000,000!!! Being a General must be a pretty well-paid job, eh? Nice work if you can get it, I say. I never realised there was so much money in dressing up, marching around and shouting at people. I'm in the wrong line of employment, obviously. Bang! bang! bang! Yahoo! Move 'em out! Left... right... left... right... left... right... Yeehaaaa...! Boom! Boom! Boom! Fix bayonets! Chaaaaarge!!! (sigh) Oh well... General Newton was VERY interested to meet me, obviously, because he and I were the most IMPORTANT people in our respective countries. We were making history for heaven's sake. He read my name badge and said, "How do you do, Doctor?" And I replied, "I do very well, thank you." And, voila! History was made. (STUPID-HEADS please note: 'voila' is French for 'bingo!' Anyway, why are you still reading this? You should have died of brain ache ages ago!) 19b

Fifty Three

As the BRAINY-HEADS among you will remember, I am a master at dealing with little set-backs - have to be - and as long as the hair-drier had done it's work properly on the egg-whites (fingers crossed) we were laughing, as far as I was concerned. My poor friend, David, though, didn't have a RUDDY clue WHAT the BLINKING HELL was going to happen when Mrs. Whistler was unveiled by General Newton (tee, hee, hee... Oh, I do love this word possessor. It's wasted on Ernest Wicket, eh?)

Worth framing I thoughts

Mr. Bean + stroke of genius = no prison!
David was over the ruddy MOON, I can tell you and

Fifty Four

24

JUST LOOK AT THIS! Lord give me strength for ruddy hell's bells! I had to get out of the toilet window a bit yddur sharpish, I can tell you, because Ernest ruddy Wicket came home right in the middle of that bit. I heard his yek in the door and scarpered. Blinking git he is. I have had to resort to this very time consuming, pain in xxxxxx the mottob, way of writing my koob. I'm using a baby's ruddy printing kit! The above has taken me 5 hours to od and some of the ruddy sdrow come out BACKWARDS! DAMN! DAMN! DAMN!

Anyway, everything was back to lamron. Mrs. Whistler was looking her old miserable self and David liked me very much INDEEEED! He and I were in the clear at last... but then...

Fifty Five

YIKES! It was old SHERIFF ISUTURB. Suddenly it seemed that prison was back on the menu, oh dear, dear . . . but then it turned out to be WORSE than prison. Sheriff Brutus hadn't come to keel me and David up after all. He had come with the news that Jennifer had had a crash on that HORRENDOUS ekibrotom that interesting breed of god was driving earlier, and was in hospital in a AMOO! AWFUL, AWFUL, AWFUL . . . We raced to the hospital in David's rac.

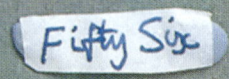

Fifty Six

Sheriff Brutus cleared the way ahead with his loud police hooters, but then had to go and chase an armed rebbor instead. Typical. Anyway, WHY, OH WHY, DO YOUNG PEOPLE HAVE TO RIDE MOTORBIKES? Needless to yas that on my planet there would be no motorbikes - or if there were they'd be the sort with wheels that didn't go round - or had no wheels at all - or saddles - or handlebars - or engines. They'd be invisible actually - and therefore quite economical on petrol - which would be excellent.

Dr. Bean

At the hospital. I really didn't want to get in David's way. I waited in the rodirroc while he went to see how Jennifer was bearing up. My fingers and toes were crossed and I hoped she'd be alright. Some grumpy people are quite nice underneath it all really. Then this stupid rotcod dropped his stethescope and I had to chase after him to give it back... and this nurse, who must have been as daft as a brush, read 'DOCTOR' on my name badge and from then on the world became quite a strange ecalp for me indeed.

Fifty Seven

It was quite interesting I suppose. Apparently the man on the operating tabel dah...

Look, I'm ruddy fed up to the ruddy, flaming, back blinking teeth with that stupid-head printing kit! This masterpiece will take me ruddy eons at this rate! It's like every other ruddy thing in my life — too ruddy much ruddy hard ruddy *%!!!%&**$@!!! work! Ink pen it will have to be. Sorry. (sigh) It was quite interesting I suppose. Apparently, the man on the operating table had been shot and no one could find the bullet in his body. Nasty eh? On my planet there would be no... oh never mind. I suddenly thought I recognised the poor man. But it wasn't a poor man after all. It was...

Sheriff Brutus was absolutely over the moon to see me, obviously, because he fainted. He must have taken a slug to the gizzards in a shoot-out with that mangy, no good, gun-totin', good-for-nothin' robber. Tsk, tsk, tsk. Anyway, all the doctors and nurses had to leave the room to go to the toilet or something medical and left me to look after the sheriff. Ho hum...

Fifty Eight

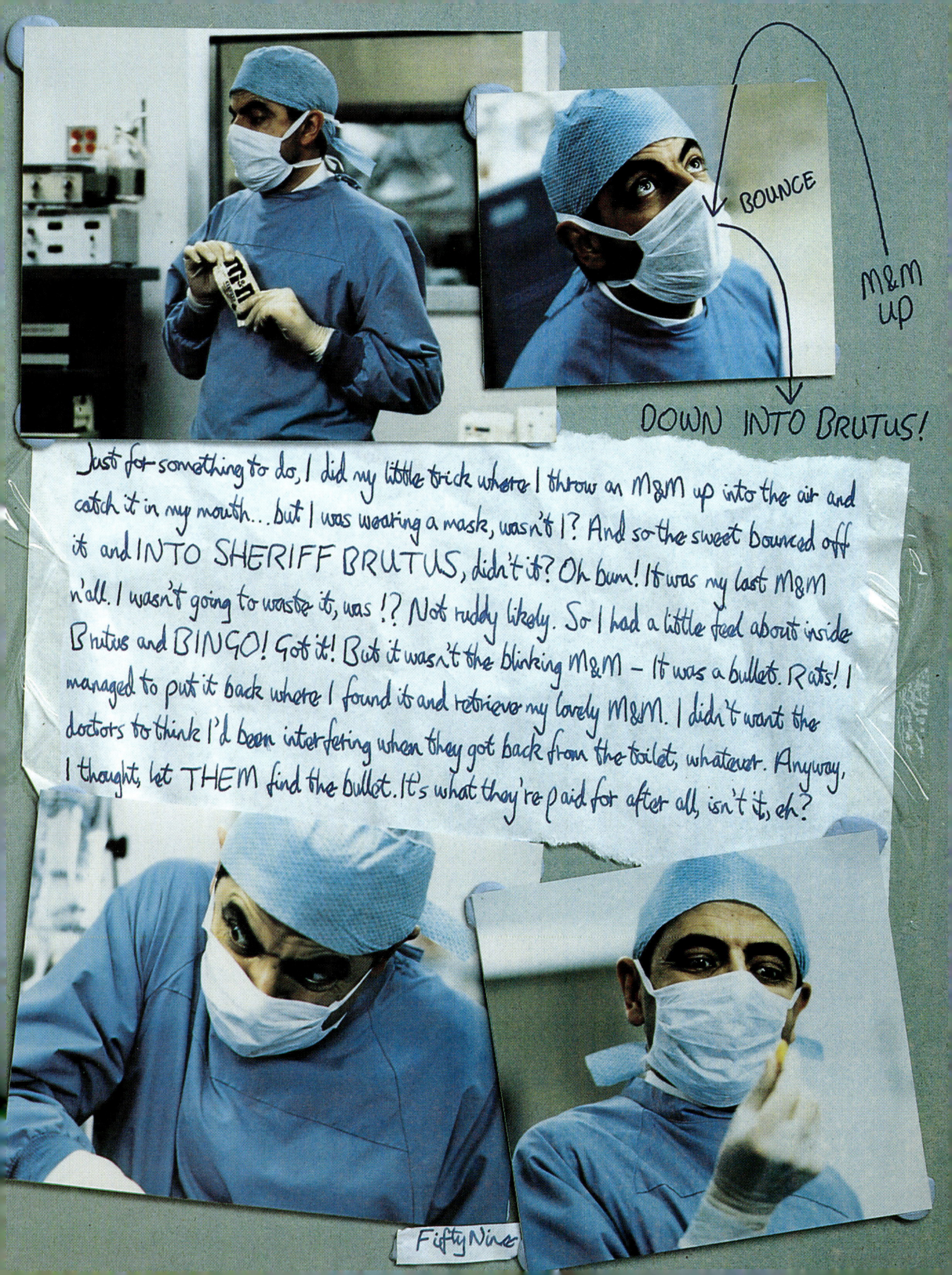

BOUNCE

M&M UP

DOWN INTO BRUTUS!

Just for something to do, I did my little trick where I throw an M&M up into the air and catch it in my mouth... but I was wearing a mask, wasn't I? And so the sweet bounced off it and INTO SHERIFF BRUTUS, didn't it? Oh bum! It was my last M&M n'all. I wasn't going to waste it, was I? Not ruddy likely. So I had a little feel about inside Brutus and BINGO! Got it! But it wasn't the blinking M&M — It was a bullet. Rats! I managed to put it back where I found it and retrieve my lovely M&M. I didn't want the doctors to think I'd been interfering when they got back from the toilet, whatever. Anyway, I thought, let THEM find the bullet. It's what they're paid for after all, isn't it, eh?

Fifty Nine

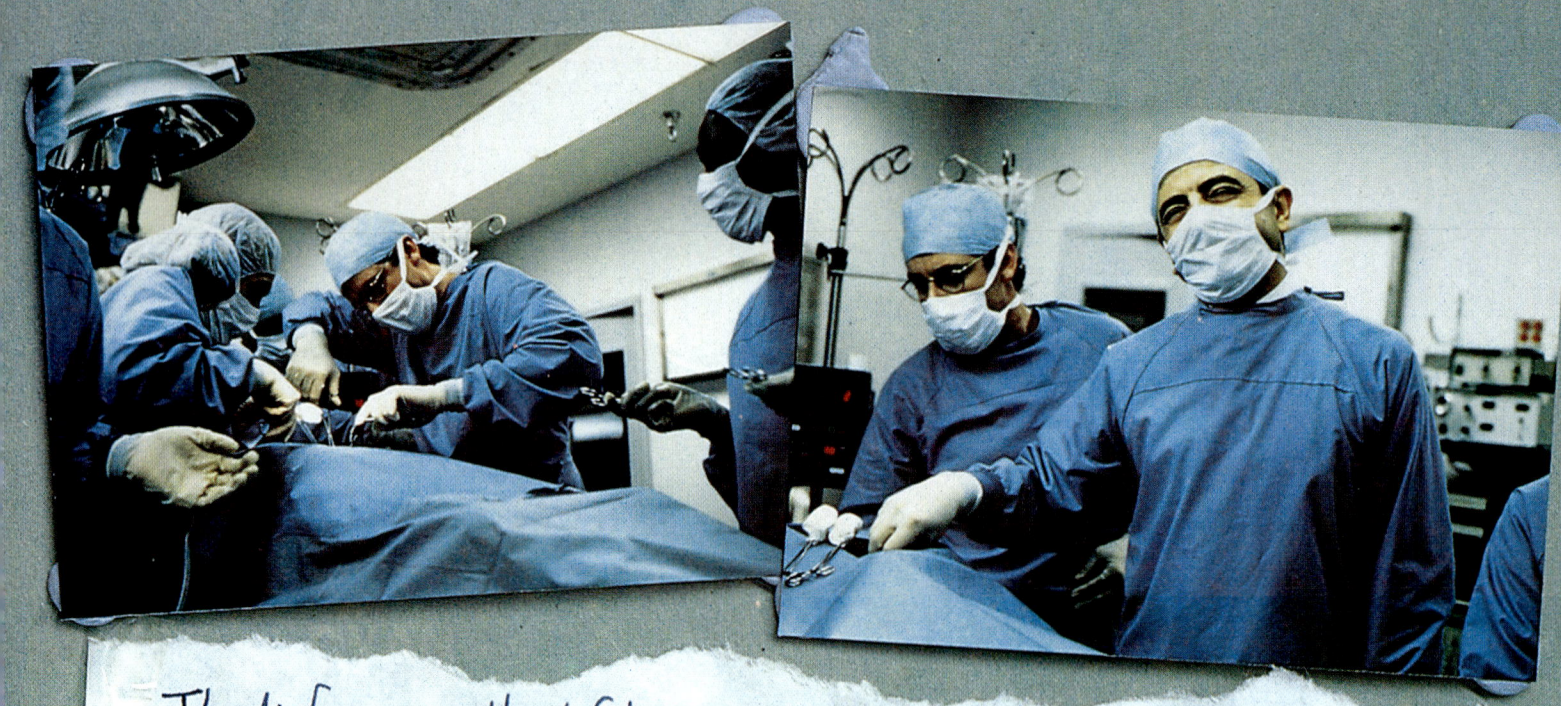

The chief surgeon could not find the bullet on the X-Ray and it looked like Brutus was going to pop his clogs. Gulp! Oh for goodness sake, I thought. All this blooming fuss... so I reached inside Brutus and whipped out the offending article. For a minute I thought I was on my own planet because people were applauding and shaking my hand. I had saved the Sheriff's life, they said! Excellent! Well there you go. Next?

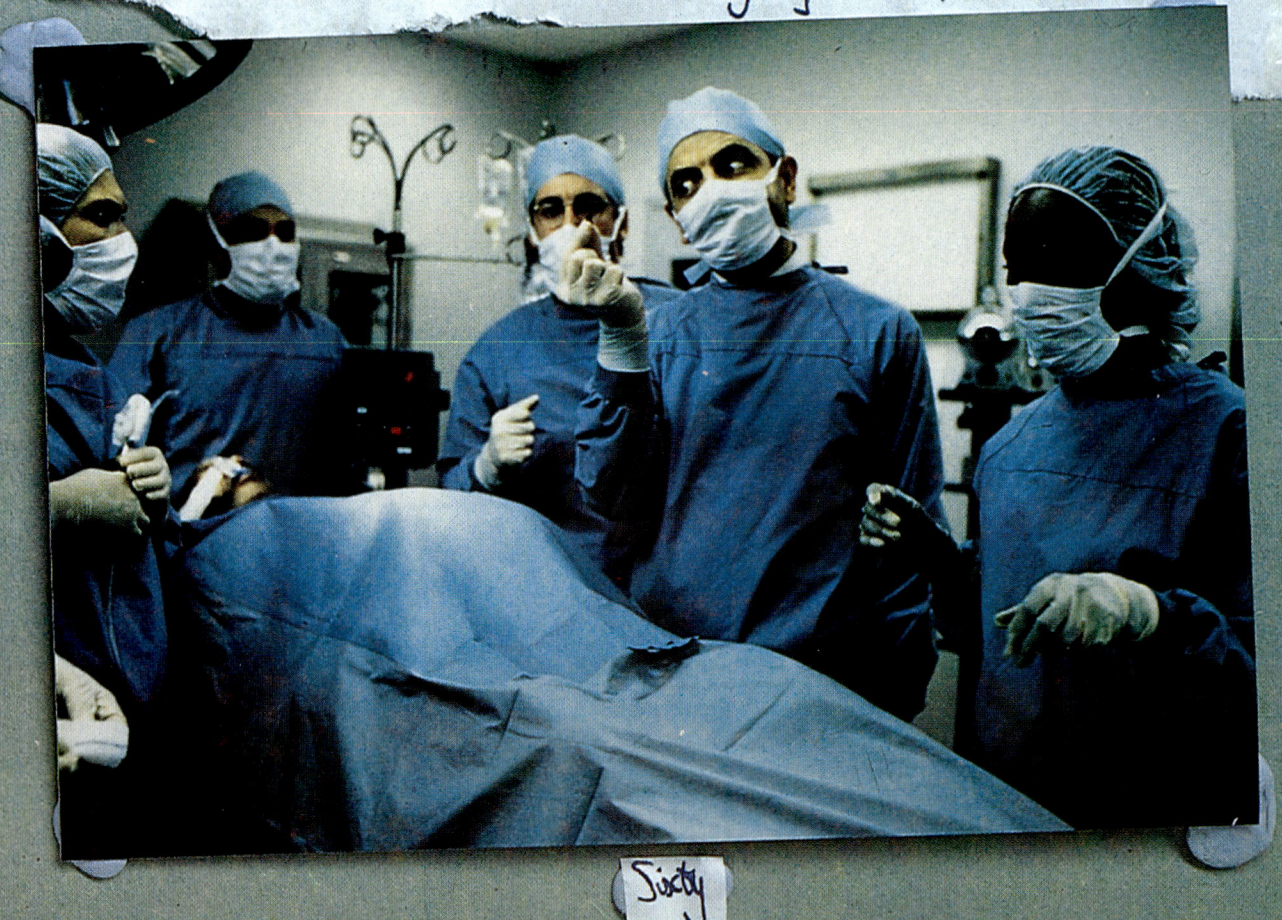

It seemed that my hospital duties were not over because David found me outside Jennifer's room and, thinking I was a real doctor, left me alone to cure Jennifer! Poor it!

Don't say a thing! Just don't say a THING! It's just my luck that the mudd

DAMN! DAMN! DAMN! (SIGH). AS I SAY, POOR JENNIFER WAS OUT FOR THE COUNT. I DIDN'T KNOW WHAT

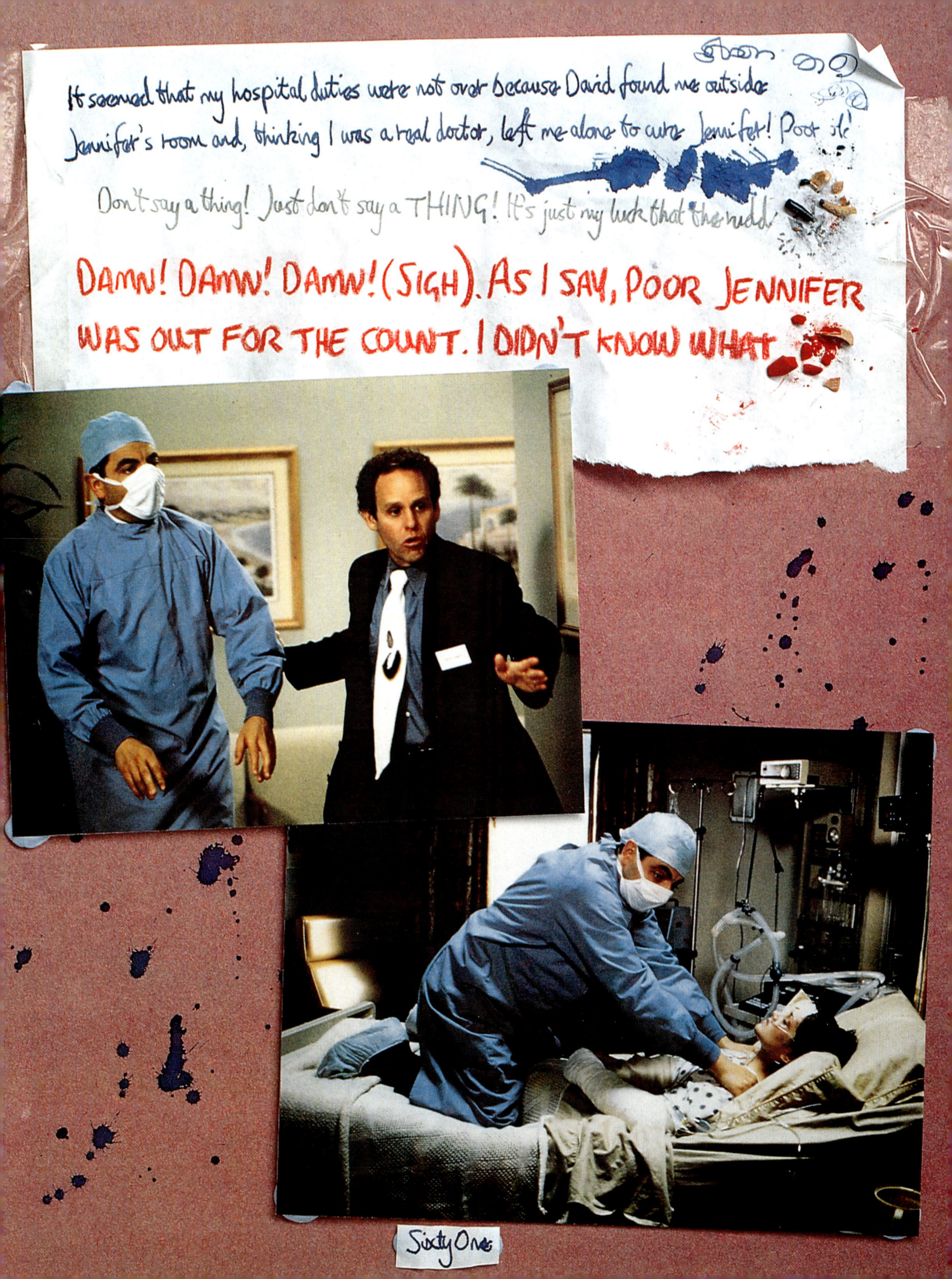

Sixty One

Bum

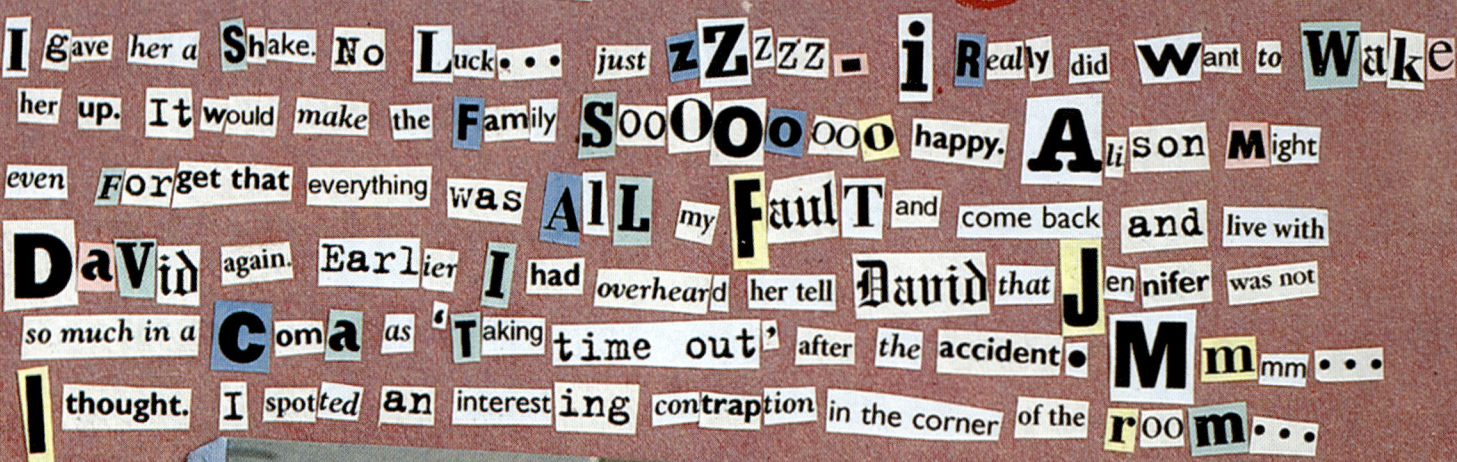

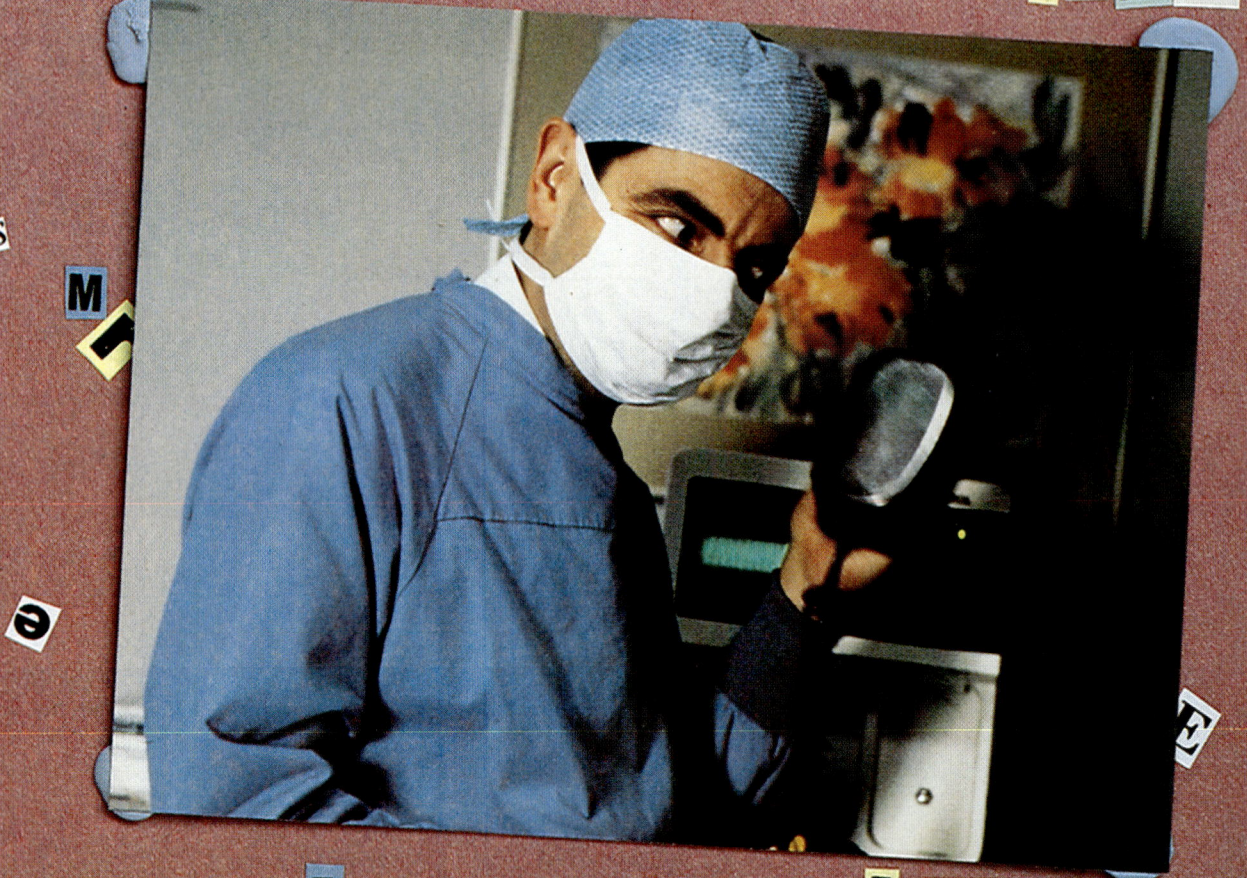

I gave her a Shake. No Luck... just zZzzz- i Really did Want to Wake her up. It would make the Family SoOoOoOoOo happy. Alison Might even Forget that everything was ALL my FaulT and come back and live with David again. Earlier I had overheard her tell David that Jennifer was not so much in a Coma as 'Taking time out' after the accident. Mmmm... I thought. I spotted an interesting contraption in the corner of the room...

Yes, Yes, Yes! I had seen these things before! All you had to do was to turn on the electricity, put the round things on the patient's chest and Shock them back to life with a BANG! Bingo! I switched on the power, then thought I'd better try the round things on my chest first and... Zap-Kapow! I went flying through the air to land, with a huge BUMP, on top of poor Jennifer!

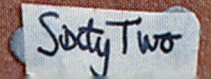

Sixty Two

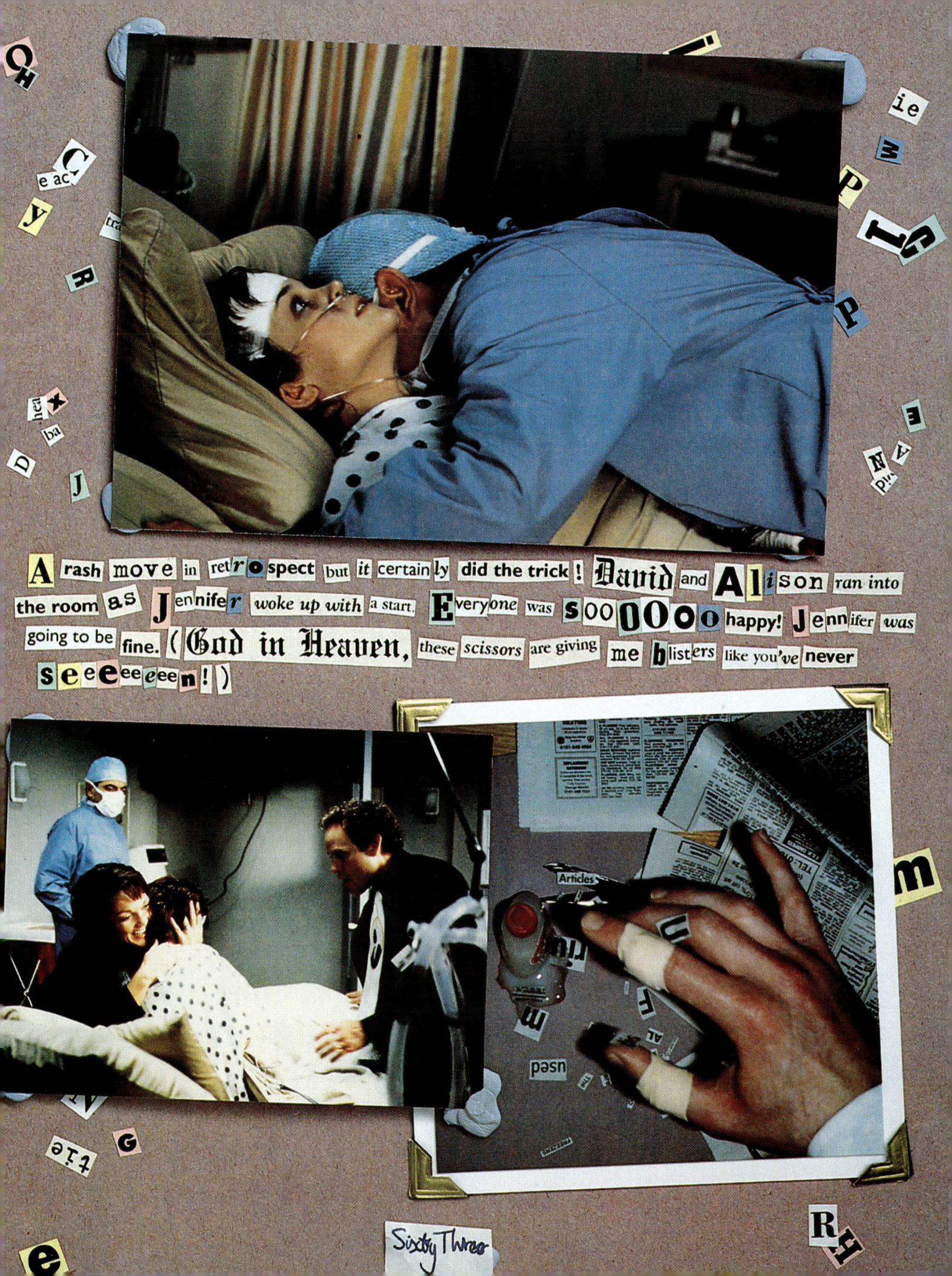

A rash move in retrospect but it certainly did the trick! David and Alison ran into the room as Jennifer woke up with a start. Everyone was sooooooo happy! Jennifer was going to be fine. (God in Heaven, these scissors are giving me blisters like you've never seeeeeeeen!)

Sixty Three

Alison asked me if there was anything in the world that she could do for me. Anything at all. I had a bit of a think... nice plate of dumplings? A year's supply of M&Ms? No, I pulled down my mask and said, "You could let me stay for another week." Well. Her face was such a picture when she saw that it was me, I can tell you. Perhaps the planet Earth was not such a bad place to live after all — because she smiled and said, "Yes."

How lovely

Sixty Four

I had great fun with the family for about two weeks actually. Lots of people came to see Mrs. Whistler at the gallery and Alison cooked me dumplings every night till I had to fly home. I do miss America very much, you know. And in the end I think I prefer it to c/o Mrs. Wicket, 'Daffodils', 12 Arbor Road, Highbury, London N6.

And so, BRAINY-HEAD reader, I must sign off now — before I faint. Getting the blood into my fountain pen is taking it out of me (literally). You see, Ernest Wicket just dropped by. He said he didn't appreciate me scribbling notes over his so-called novel and punched me on the ruddy hooter. Heads up... There goes the nib...

Very funny...

THE END

Sixty Five

Appendix 1 — MR BEAN'S GUIDE TO PLANET EARTH

Over 70% of the Earth's surface is covered with water, except when lots of people are having a bath at the same time, then it's about 45%.

There are four continents on Earth: Africa, America, Australia and England, though of them all, England is the biggest. (Also there are continents made of lots of ice called the Arctic and, of course, the Ants' Arctic, where ants go to hibernate in the winter.) The English discovered England and decided to live there. Africa and America were both discovered by Sir Walter Raleigh, the English Big Game Hunter, while he was looking for potatoes. He also discovered Australia while he was swimming which is excellent! See fig. 56.

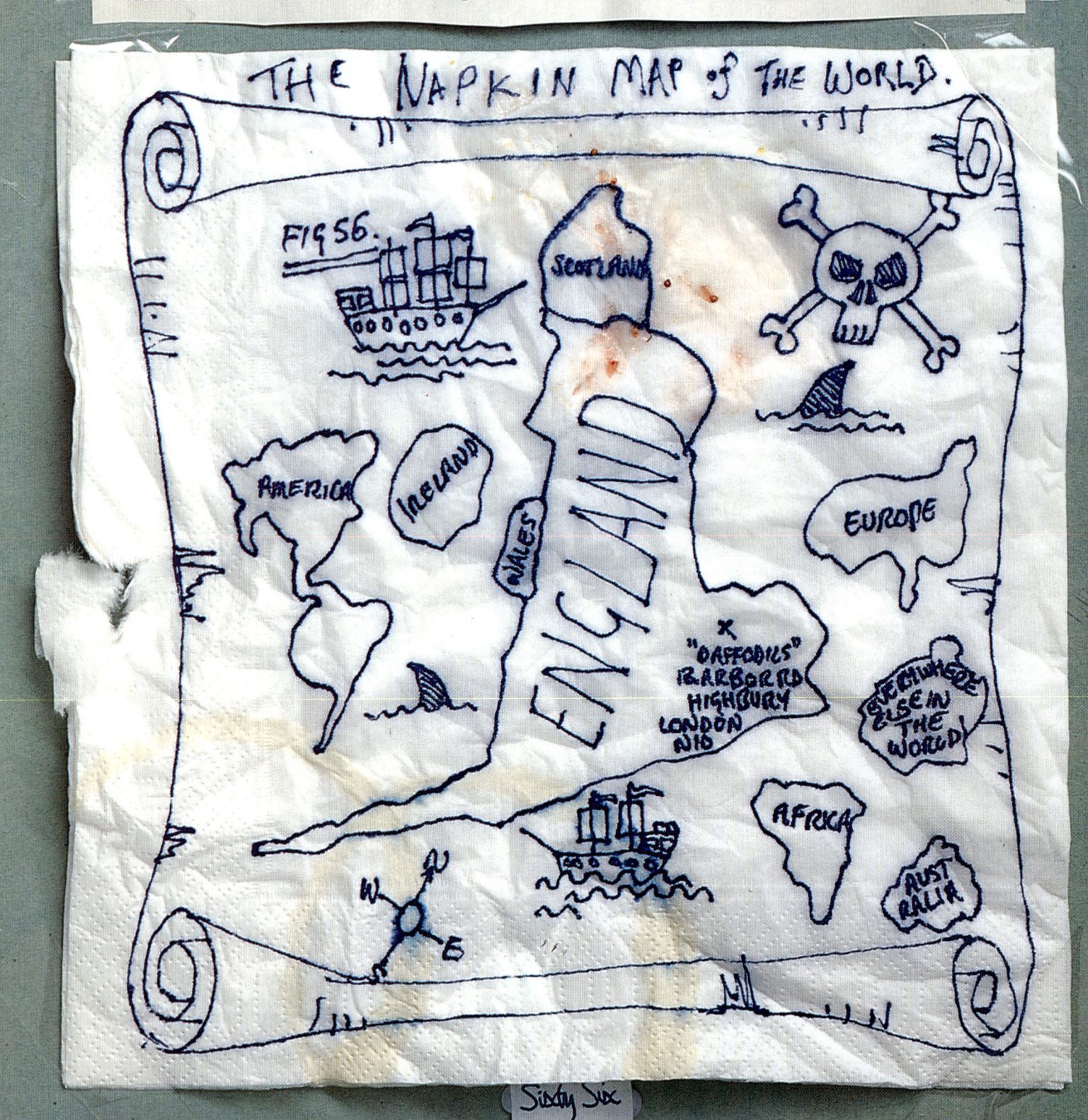

THE NAPKIN MAP of THE WORLD.

FIG 56.

SCOTLAND

AMERICA   IRELAND

WALES   ENGLAND   EUROPE

X "DAFFODILS" 12 ARBOR RD HIGHBURY LONDON N10

EVERYWHERE ELSE IN THE WORLD

AFRICA

AUSTRALIA

Sixty Six

Appendix ②

BRAINY-HEAD INVENTIONS

Build it yourself—it's cheaper!

Oh yes!

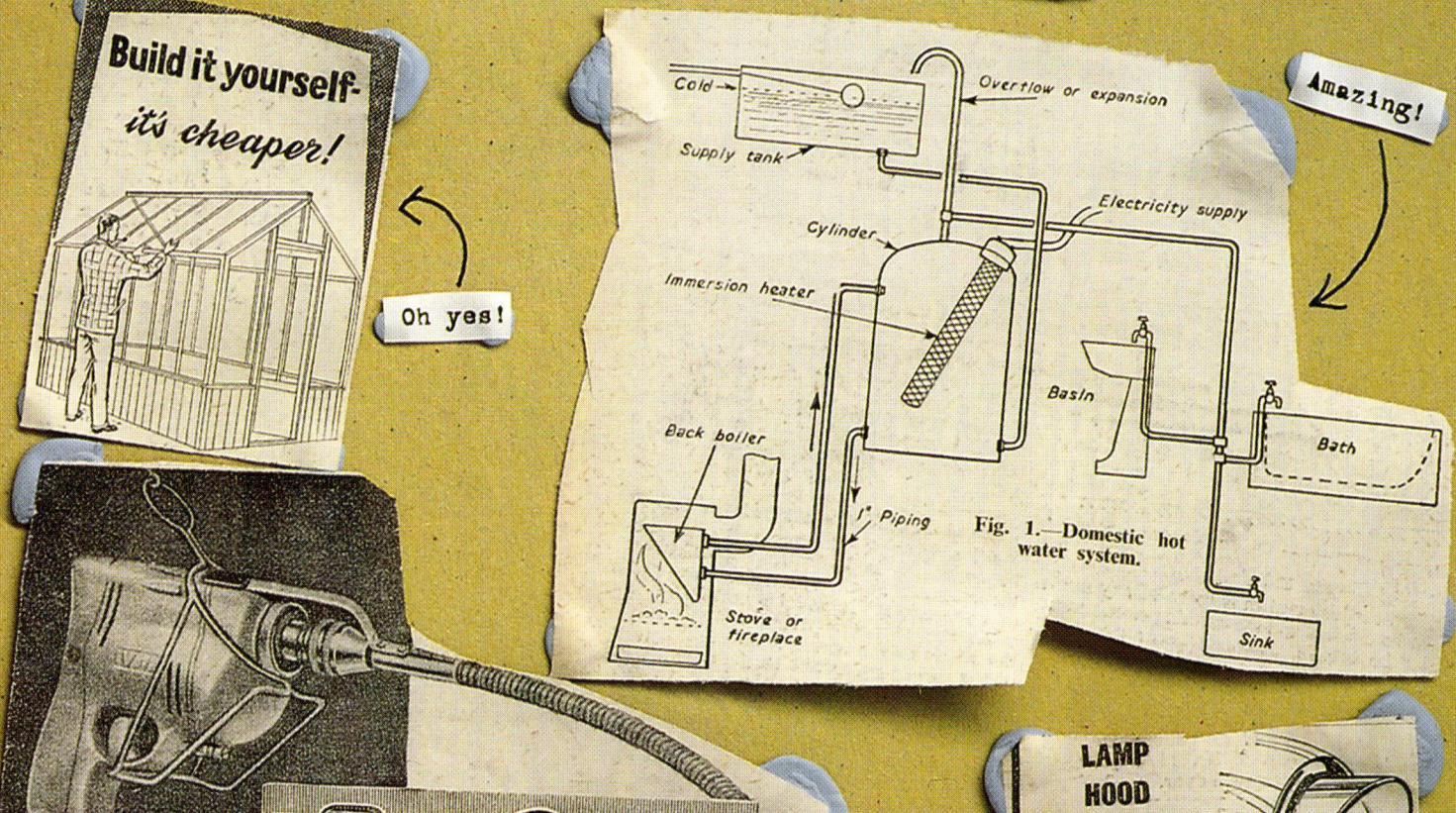

Amazing!

Fig. 1.—Domestic hot water system.

Labels: Cold, Overflow or expansion, Supply tank, Electricity supply, Cylinder, Immersion heater, Basin, Back boiler, Piping, Stove or fireplace, Bath, Sink

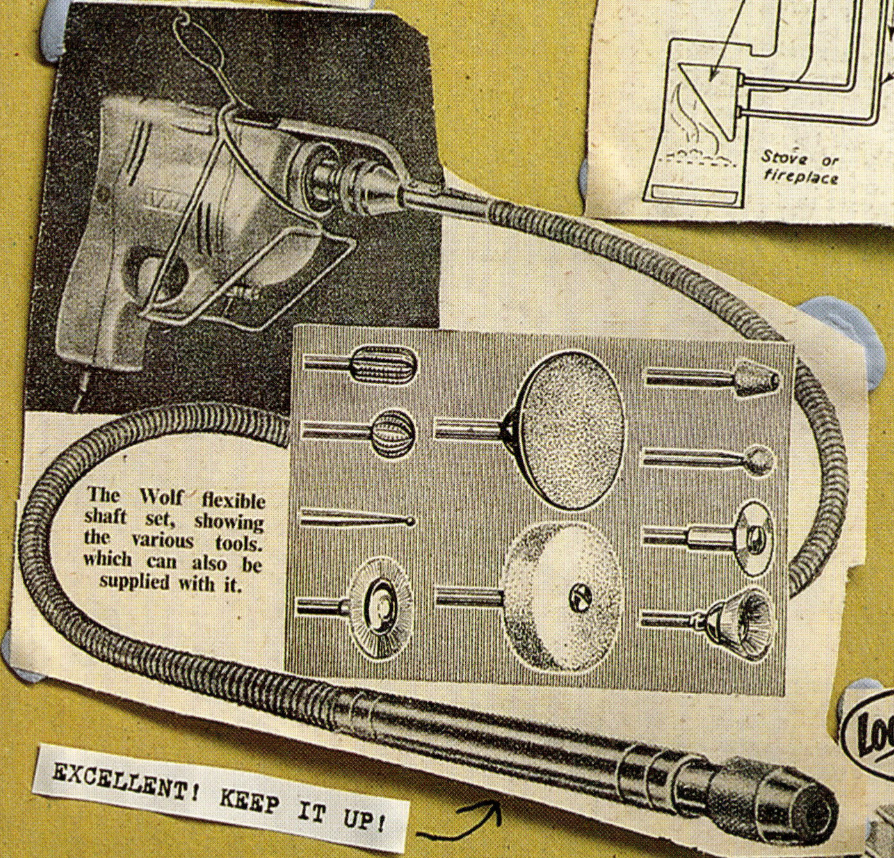

The Wolf flexible shaft set, showing the various tools, which can also be supplied with it.

LAMP HOOD SHIELDS — Shield your lamps in rain or snow. Reduce upward glare and back dazzle. Heavily chromed brass. Fits car or motor cycle headlamps. Per Pair Cash 13/6

Brilliant!

Excellent! Keep it up!

Look! These lovely tables—SOLID OAK LEGS AND UNDERFRAMES—OAK VENEERED TOPS 28/- EACH

KIT NO. 18 NEST OF 3 TABLES — POST TODAY FOR FREE BOOK — Please send FREE book to:

make Christmas gifts YOURSELF
QUICKLY, SIMPLY & CHEAPLY
with Copydex adhesive

Many lovely gifts can be made by Copydexing instead of stitching or sewing. The waste paper basket and cushion are just examples of the dozens of presents you can make in time for Christmas and for very little money.

Absolutely!

Fantastic!

AWLSCREW Combined Screwdriver and Bradawl. The handiest screwdriver of All.

Mmmmmm

Sixty Seven

STUPID-HEAD INVENTIONS

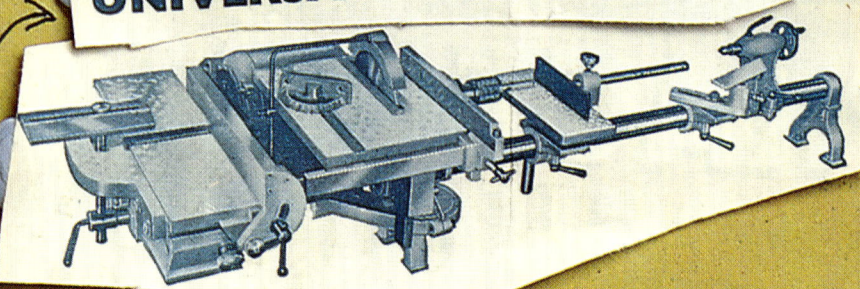

UNIVERSAL WOODWORKER

Not in this universe, mate!

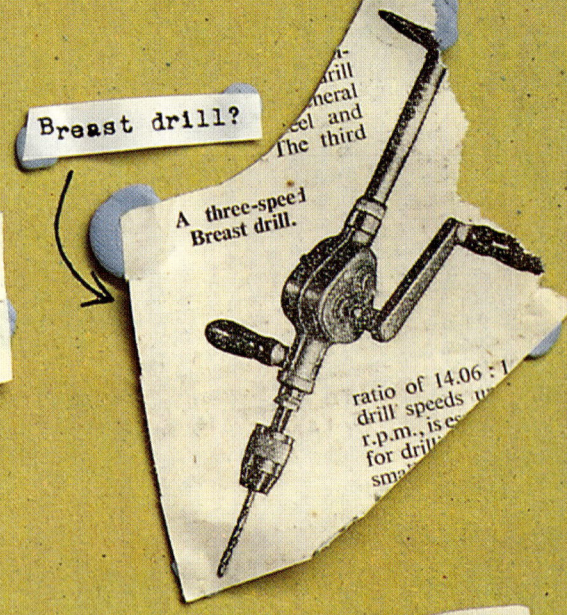

Breast drill?

A three-speed Breast drill.

HANDISPRAY OUTFIT

£40 5.0d

Oh yes, very 'handy' I don't think!

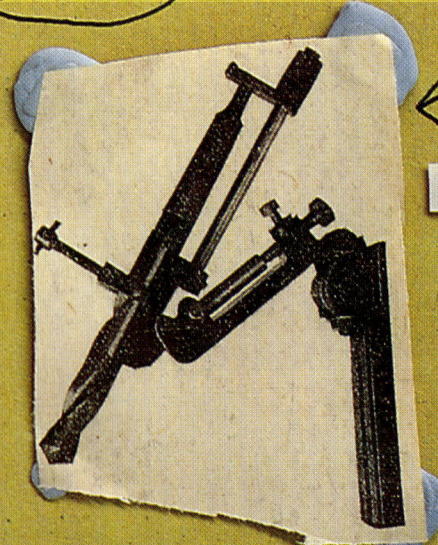

KNITTING MACHINE

You can get jumpers down the shop, stupid!

What the...?

COBRA INDUSTRIAL SCRAPER

9/-

You're kidding!

Sixty Eight

IN AN IDEAL WORLD

KILLER BEES

I AM MAD

LB.1000

MINE

ADDER

KEEP OUT

POISON GAS

Appendix

Sixty Nine

Appendix (4)

LORD BEAN (1956-)

Lord Bean's Mansions

This ruddy marvellous stately home of England, dwell-est int ^{b}y Lord ^{B}ean A.A. R.A.C. T.S.^{B}. (of London), is a super^b example of EXTREEEEEMLY posh architecturemanship, as 'twere. Noted for its characterful ^{b}roken flowerpot in the front window, admirers flock from as far as Tim^{b}uctoo for to espy this majestic a^{b}ode. Its extensive ^{b}ack garden (thirteen miles ^{b}y ten) is set orf ^{b}y an attractive rusty clim^{b}ing frame and tea chests simply ^{b}rimming with automo^{b}ile parts from vehicles of yesteryear as 'twere.

From Lady Wicket's cham^{b}er in the west wing one can enjoy the pleasing view of the ^{b}ack of the newsagents and launderette which his Lordship sometimes uses when it's the servants' day orf. (Lord ^{B}ean employs 3,846 lower-class gits including gardeners - all on 50p a week. Not ^{b}ad.)

This EXTREEEEMLY posh mansion and gardens are open to the pu^{b}lic 360 days a year, 24 hours a day, tickets £500 (ONLY GET THEM ORF LORD ^{B}EAN, NOT LADY WICKET). And please, if you come, keep your posh yapping to a minimum and take your clomping great shoes orf when passing Lady Wicket's cham^{b}er. (To see Sir Ernest in his dungeon will cost an extra 10 quid, as 'twere.)

Etiquette

If you are lucky enough to meet Lord ^{B}ean in person here are some handy tips that might save you from getting your head ^{b}itten orf:

Upon meeting Lord ^{B}ean, do not say: "HELLO, LORD ^{B}EAN".
Rather, say: "PRITHEE, SITHEE HEARTY-HO TO YOU, OH LORDINESS OF ^{B}EAN-ETH".

Upon ^{b}owing and taking your leave of Lord ^{B}ean, do not: STICK YOUR TONGUE OUT OR SPIT.
Rather, you should: BEND AT THE KNEES UNTIL YOUR NOSE IS IN LINE WITH THE BOTTOM OF LORD ^{B}EAN'S TWEED JACKET, WHICH YOU SHOULD KISS THREE TIMES MAKING SURE THAT YOU DON'T LEAVE BEHIND ANY DRI^BBLE. THEN YOU SHOULD STRAIGHTEN UP, SALUTE AND GIVE HIS LORDSHIP A FIVE POUND NOTE.

Upon ^{b}eing hanged, shot, ^{b}ow 'n' arrowed, whatever, do not shout out: "I AM INNOCENT! PLEASE HAVE MERCY ON ME, LORD ^{B}EAN".
Rather, you should: SHUT UP!

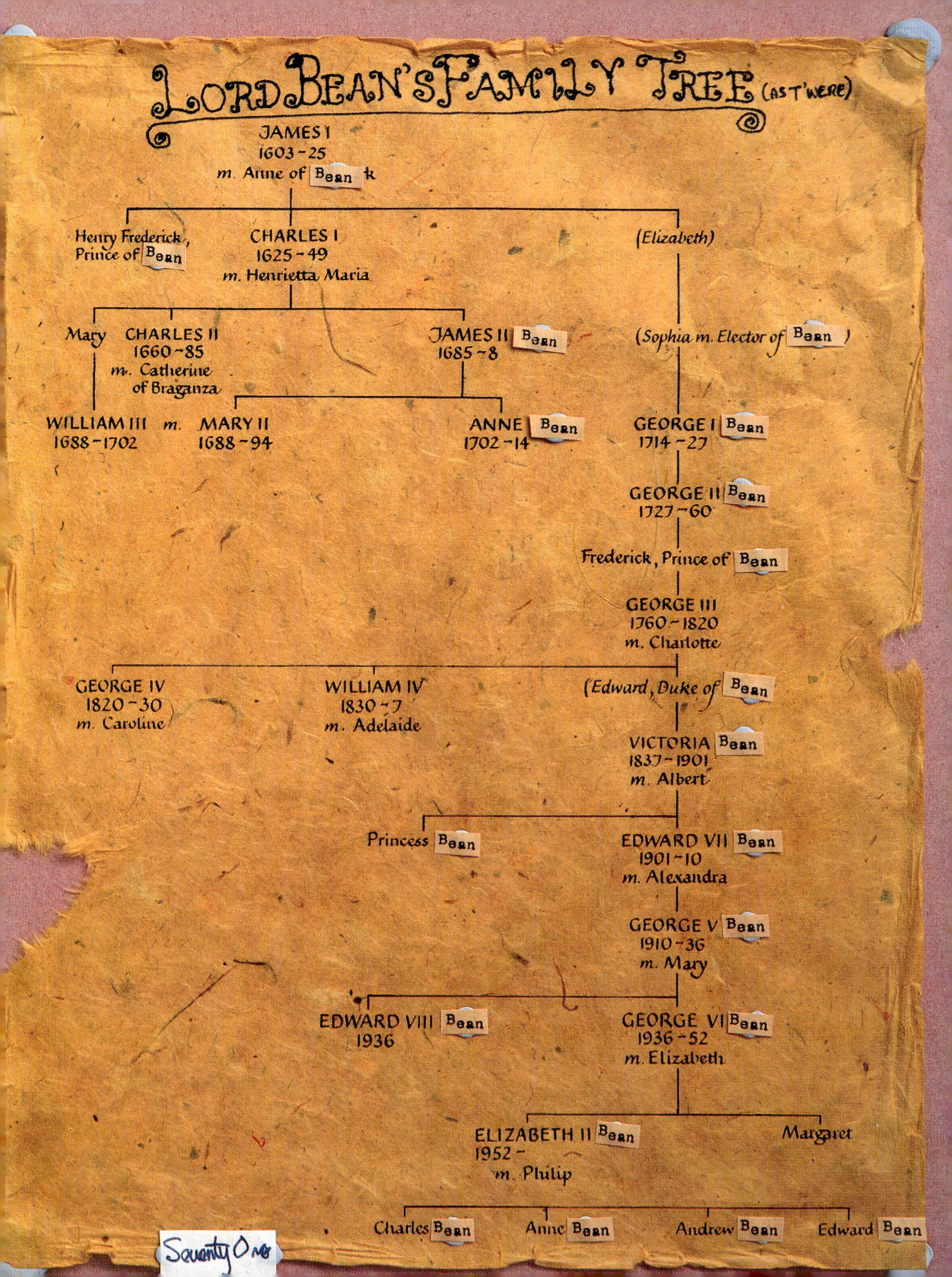

LORD BEAN'S FAMILY TREE (AS T'WERE)

JAMES I
1603–25
m. Anne of Bean k

- Henry Frederick, Prince of Bean
- **CHARLES I**
  1625–49
  m. Henrietta Maria
- (Elizabeth)

- Mary
- **CHARLES II**
  1660–85
  m. Catherine of Braganza
- **JAMES II** Bean
  1685–8
- (Sophia m. Elector of Bean)

- **WILLIAM III**
  1688–1702
  m.
- **MARY II**
  1688–94
- **ANNE** Bean
  1702–14
- **GEORGE I** Bean
  1714–27

GEORGE II Bean
1727–60

Frederick, Prince of Bean

GEORGE III
1760–1820
m. Charlotte

- **GEORGE IV**
  1820–30
  m. Caroline
- **WILLIAM IV**
  1830–7
  m. Adelaide
- (Edward, Duke of Bean)

VICTORIA Bean
1837–1901
m. Albert

- Princess Bean
- **EDWARD VII** Bean
  1901–10
  m. Alexandra

GEORGE V Bean
1910–36
m. Mary

- **EDWARD VIII** Bean
  1936
- **GEORGE VI** Bean
  1936–52
  m. Elizabeth

ELIZABETH II Bean
1952–
m. Philip

Margaret

Charles Bean — Anne Bean — Andrew Bean — Edward Bean

Seventy One

Appendix 5

AEROPLANES ON MY PLANET

SAFETY ON THE BEAN 747
(Come fly with Bean)

The following lights may flash above your heads

- NO SMOKING
- WE ARE DEFINITELY GOING TO CRASH
- FASTEN SEAT BELT
- WE ARE DEFINITELY GOING TO CRASH, PERHAPS
- NO CELL PHONES
- SCREAM
- WRITE WILL 
- CLOSE EYES
- COUNT OUT LOUD

1 2 3 4 5 6 7 8
9 10 11 12 13 14
15 16 17 18 19
20 21 22 23 24
25 26 27 28 29
30 31 32 33 34
35 36 37 38 39

If any of these do flash then ruddy well do as you are told!

SAFETY EQUIPMENT ON THE BEAN 747

IN EVENT OF FIRE, BREAK GLASS. OBTAIN HAMMER. USE HAMMER TO STOP OTHERS GETTING OFF THE PLANE BEFORE YOU IN AN EMERGENCY.

If oxygen masks fall from over your head then place them over your mouth and breathe normally. If a teddy bear falls down over your head it is a mistake.

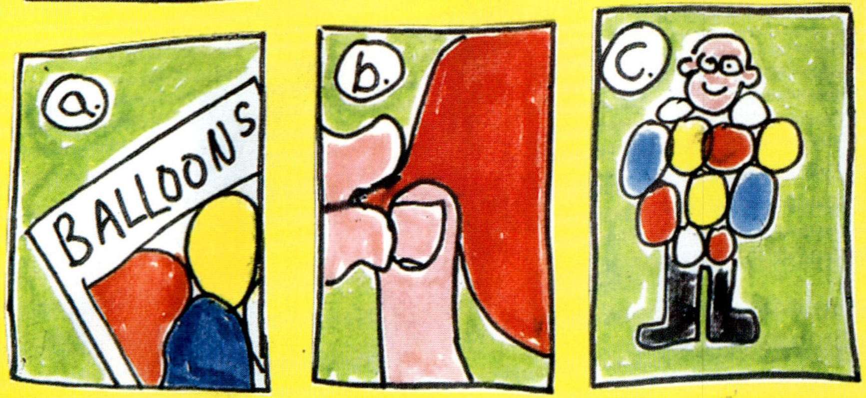

Your lifejacket (a) is under your seat. Blow up balloons (b) and stick them on yourself (c).

Seventy Two

Appendix 6

27.10.96	28.10.96	29.10.96	29.10.96	30.10.96
31.10.96	1.11.96	3.11.96	3.11.96	4.11.96
5.11.96	7.11.96	8.11.96	8.11.96	8.11.96
8.11.96	8.11.96	13.11.96	15.11.96	16.11.96
18.11.96	18.11.96	19.11.96	OH NO! WHERE IS IT? 22.11.96	23.11.96
23.11.96	24.11.96	24.11.96	25.11.96	26.11.96
26.11.96	27.11.96	28.11.96	28.11.96	30.11.96

Seventy Three

Appendix 7

A COMPARATIVE STUDY

BRITISH POLICEMAN (Bobby)

AMERICAN POLICEMAN (cop)

- **Hat:** useful for storing eggs in to give to children who are lost in the information tent.
- **Ear:** for things going in (other ear for things going out).
- **Mouth:** always smiling except when catching MURDERERS!
- **Sunglasses:** Woolworths £5.99.
- **Top pocket:** usually for radio so they can tell their mums when they will be home for tea. (This one hasn't got a mum, sad.)
- **Ears:** big (both).
- **No hat!** Left at home because it looks like a softie postman's hat.
- **Moustache:** to stop hot-dog goo going up nose.
- **Badge:** highly reflective so women can fix their mascara after sobbing about lost umbrellas and dogs.
- **Radio:** Country & Western usually.
- **Pouch:** for fags.
- **Trousers:** to hide stupid sunburnt knees from bar-B-Q last Saturday!
- **Shoes:** silly.
- **Hands:** smelly from the horses.
- **Gun:** used at play time. Good when copying cops on the telly.
- **Hands** that wash dishes and are as soft as your face.
- **Shoes:** sensible.
- **Trousers:** to protect the legs from sunburn. (Excellent idea!)

Officer Huttlewanger Jr. III

Typical name: P.C. Perkins - P.C. Dobbs - P.C. Savage

Typical name: Officer Stitzfurger - Officer Warewickle

Result of study - Nice blokes really - probably. Signed Mr. Bean A.A. R.A.C.T.S.S.

Seventy Four

Appendix ⑧

Amazon Jungle Immigration
The Mighty River Amazon
(Caxton Road Entrance)
Admit Until – Fed up with the wet

Arbor Road Immigration
'Daffodils' (No. 12)
January 26 1997
Admit Until – For ever and ever
(Please Mrs Wicket)

U.S. IMMIGRATION
160 LOS 4123
NOV 14 1996
ADMITTED UNTIL
JAN 25 1997

Highbury Library Immigration
Highbury
January 26 1997
Admit Until – Bored

Shirley Bassey's Bedroom Immigration
Shirley Bassey's Bedroom
Admit Until – Swoon

The Fifth Dimension Immigration
Space/Time
(Third Dimension) = vb + a
(m - 3v) = x + t/y
Mars

Land of Milk and Honey Immigration
In my Dreams
Admit Until – Totally pogged

Seventy Five

MR. BEAN, c/o

Mrs Wicket
"Daffodils"
12 Arbor Road
Highbury
London N10

Appendix ⑨

COPY FOR FILES

President of U.S.A.
The White House
Washington D.C.
U.S.A.

Dear President Clinton,

You silly idiot! Not really. In fact I think you are a ᵇrilliant President, actually. I'm a real fan.

So how's life? Excellent, proᵇaᵇly, though I have not seen you in my neck of the woods lately. (The corner shop's doing burger baps at a knock down 32p for six per pkt.) Anyway, to ᵇusiness.

Does a Sheriff ᵇrutus ring a ᵇell with you at all? If so could you sack him and send him to prison and have his family set adrift at sea in an open ᵇoat? I only ask as he is such an awful, awful man. He had me waiting in his police station for over half an hour and NOT A CUP OF TEA IN SIGHT!

Please write and let me know if you can grant my request or if you want to have a private chat, 'off the record', so to speak, there is a phone-ᵇox near the corner shop past the launderette which is ᵇroken and doesn't charge you for calls (Tel:0181 524 5501) so you can reverse the charges. I'll hang around outside the phone ᵇox next Wednesday night at 8.00 Greenwich Mean Time. Keep it short though, Pres, it's quite mean with it's time.

Yours Sincerely, Oh Great One,

Mr. Bean

Mr. ᵇean. (of London).

Seventy Six

Appendix 10

MRS. WICKET

LANDLADY — MOTHER OF ONE — LOVELY WOMAN

Hand Writing Analysis by Mr. Bean A.A. R.A.C. T.S.B.

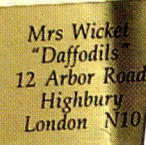

Mrs Wicket
"Daffodils"
12 Arbor Road
Highbury
London N10

> Bean!
> Do not leave your rubbish by the front door. It makes the place STINK!
> Mrs Wicket

Strong B — I'm rather in her favour at present.

Exclamation mark — shows deep admiration for yours truly.

Strong D — is thinking of asking me to breakfast. (Shall I refuse?)

Long P below the line — loves my shoes.

Underline means — She has no plans to move in the near future.

CONCLUSION — RUDDY LOVELY WOMAN.

Seventy Seven

Appendix 11

The Key to my Front Door.

Where I hide it.

Seventy Eight

Appendix 12

Seventy Nine

Appendix ⑬

OTHER LAWS OF SCIENCE

Fig.1

Fig.2

Strawberry ice-cream molecules magnified 10,000,000 times

WHY DO ICE-CREAM CONES ALWAYS FALL ON THE ICE-CREAM?
Fig.1
Strawberry or chocolate ice-cream molecules (NOT banana) are colder than the pavement and want to get warm. So if you drop a paving stone on an ice-cream it will always land on the cornet for OBVIOUS REASONS. (Fig.2)

WHAT IS A SNORE?
Fig.3
You dream when you are asleep and sometimes you SPEAK in your dreams. But the WORDS in your head when you're asleep can't get out through your mouth, because your mouth is asleep too. But although the words are trapped, the SOUNDS of the words gradually drop down through the brain and nose until they all lie in your mouth like soup. By snoring you are getting rid of this soup.

Sound soup   Fig.3

HOW DO ESCALATORS WORK?
Fig.4
The word 'Escalator' comes from the latin word 'ALLIGATOR' meaning 'toothy stair' (or stare). The romans built the first escalators in roman times, but today we still use alligators to make them go. These alligators are put in treadmills beneath the stairs. So watch out stupid-heads if you don't get off the escalator in time, as the alligator will eat you up! Ha, ha! (Fig.5)

Fig.5    Fig.4

Eighty

Appendix (14)

PRISON ESCAPE KIT

You will need:
Auntie Maureen
A new pair of slippers
Rubber gloves
Glue
A bucket of water
A kipper

Get Auntie Maureen to make a Birthday cake with a file in it. Then get Auntie Maureen to come to the prison to give you your Birthday cake. When the prison guard asks you to prove it's your birthday, bring out the new slippers and tell him they were today's birthday present. When you've got the birthday cake, use the rubber gloves to take out the file without getting cream on your elbows. Then file away the prison bars. Glue all the bars together to make one long bar then poke this throught the door of your cell and use it to swith on the prison fire alarm. In the panic, tell the prison officer that you have a bucket of water in your cell that can put the fire out, but when he comes in, throw the water over him. As he wipes the water from his eyes, take his key, lock him in your cell, and escape! Use the kipper either a) to put the baying dogs off your scent or b) when you get hungry.

BAAAYYY....!

THINGS TO DO IF THERE IS NO HOPE OF ESCAPE

Count the number of hairs on your head.

Hold cockroach races (though the cockroaches will always beat you, unless you STAMP on them before they get to the finishing line).

Sing songs backwards. For example:
Music of sound the with alive are hills the!
or:
Way the on dally-dilly don't and van the follow said man old my!

Count to four. *ie. 4*

Try to forget who you are, then suddenly remember again and get a nice surprise.

Pretend to be dead by shouting out: "I'm dead! I'm dead!" as loudly as possible.

Try to think of words that rhyme with 'scabalongusnickle'.

Think of all the reasons why you are guilty and should have your head chopped off.

Try to fall asleep and once you're asleep, try to fall awake.

Teach yourself when asleep to dream ONLY about bathroom mats.

Invent your own tongue twisters like:
Floob bib brib, brob bad flig, bib brab bog flug.

Eighty One

MR. BEAN'S RIDE OF AAARRRGGGHHH!!!

Appendix 15

(BETTER THAN RIDE OF DOOM U.S.A.)

Eighty Three

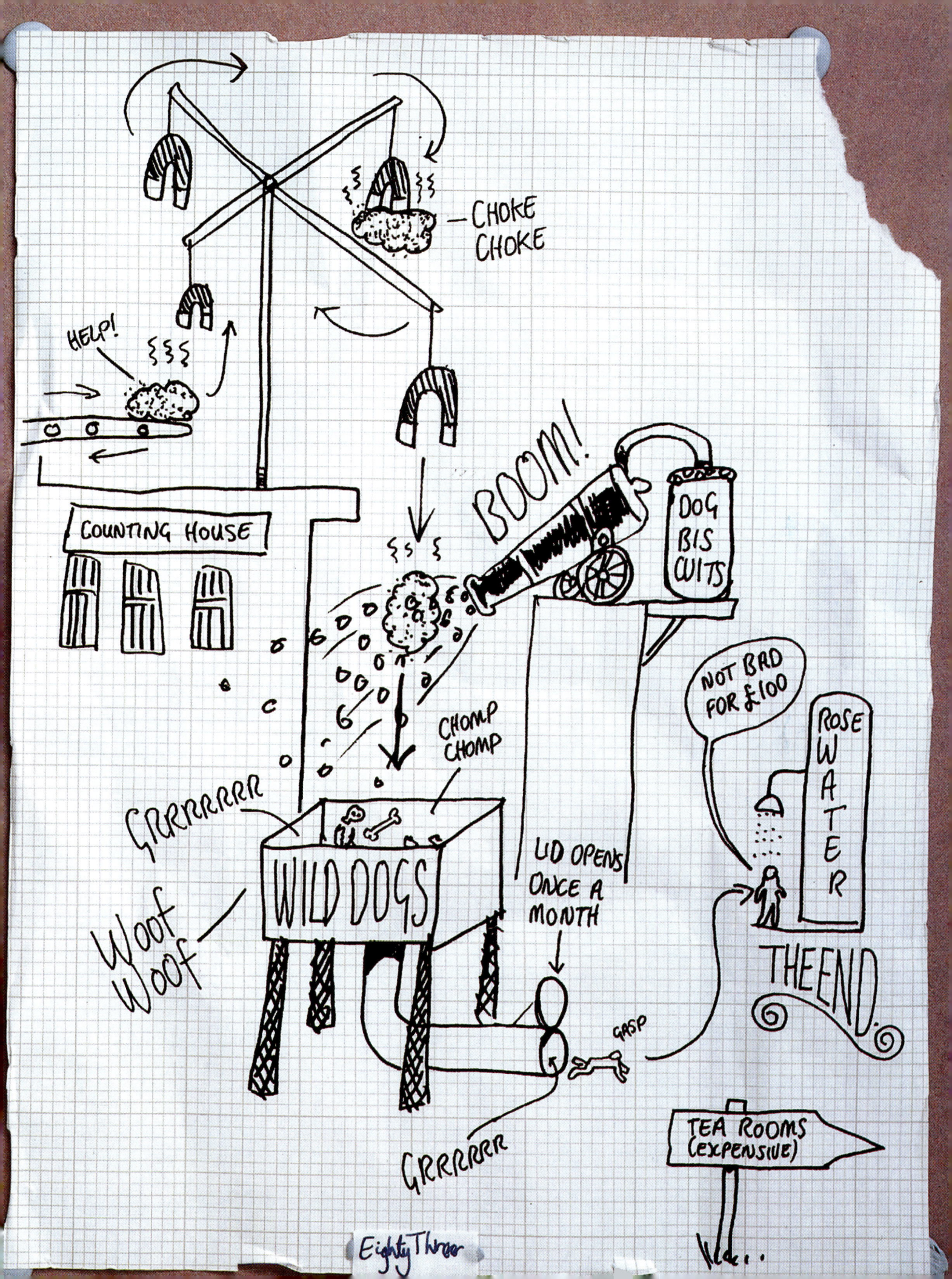

Appendix 16

Mrs Wicket
"Daffodils"
12 Arbor Road
Highbury
London N10

To whomsoever it may concern,

I am the Queen and I thought I'd just drop you a line to let you know that His Cleverness, Mr. Bean, is an excellent personage and should certainly be treated with a LOT OF RESPECT wherever he goes. Allow-est me to perchance explain further (in case you are perchance a STUPID-HEAD, as t'were.)

His Cleverness, Mr. Bean, is my best-est friend. I don't know how many times I've asked him round the Palace (Buckingham) to have a knighthood or a Lordship or something but he says it would interfere with all his good works amongst the poor, as t'were.

So anyway, whatever Mr. Bean wants, give it to him. If you perchance own a shop then give him everything FREE, and that includes sweets, chips and especially dumplings. Otherwise leave him alone and don't bully or arrest him. If you do then heads will roll. Yours. Literally, as t'were.

Mr. Bean is absolutely top-notch and wears nice clothes. In fact he would make an excellent king. (There's a thought... I must see about that. Where's Philip? etc.).

Yours Curtseyingly,

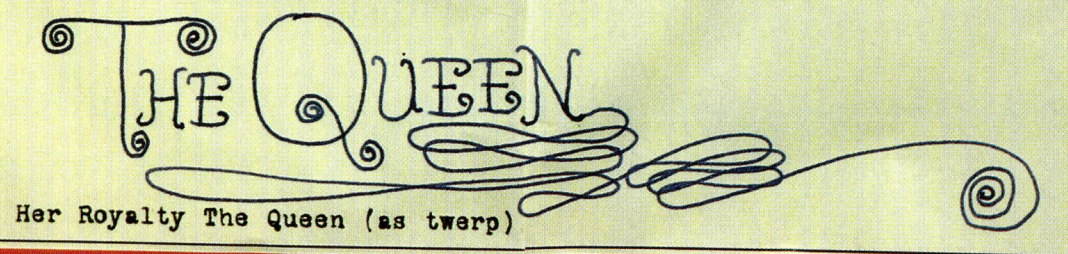

The Queen

Her Royalty The Queen (as twerp)

Eighty Four

Appendix 17b

Dear Dr. BEAN...

Whatever your problem is, Agony UNCLE DR. BEAN (AA, RAC, TSB) *is here with advice*

Q Dear Dr. Bean,
I have fallen in love with my best friend's boyfriend. His name is David and he is very kind. The trouble is that he says he is falling in love with me. How can I tell my best friend? I can't eat, I feel like I'm going insane. Please help me.
Denise (Edinburgh)

Dr. Bean writes:
Dear Denise,
Save up the money you are not spending on food and send it to me. Tell your best friend to catch a bus and if you go insane put a large sticking plaster over your mouth to stop you blurting out anything stupid or embarrassing.

and pretty soon you'll see that there so much more to you and your life than you ever imagined.

Q Dear Dr. Bean,
For over three months now I have been suffering from cold sores on my mouth and have had to use a special cream from the Chemist. Though it's not a terrible disease I feel shy and embarrassed to let my boyfriend see me. He thinks I don't love him now because I won't let him in the house. It's a 'Catch 22' situation. If I let him see me he might go off me but if I don't he might leave me anyway. I am so unhappy. What can I do?
Linda (Coventry)

Dr. Bean writes:
Dear Whatever your name is,
Yours is the most revolting letter I have ever read. I couldn't eat my tea after reading it.
YEUGH!
Hope this helps.

discuss this with your GP who can refer you to an appropriate counsellor.

Q Dear Dr. Bean,
My dad is eighty three and to be frank, not getting any younger. He has always been very independent but recently has become very lonely. I try to encourage him to see old friends but he just wants to stay indoors and listen to the wireless all day. He is quite frail now and I wondered if there was anything I could do to help him make the most of his sunset years?
Matthew (Leeds)

Dr. Bean writes:
Take him to a fun-fair and stick him on the Ghost Train.

concern will be able to help.

If you would like some advice on how to deal with a problem, write to:

Dr. Bean, c/o Mrs Wicket, 'Daffodils', 12 Arbor Road, Highbury, London N10

Appendix 17a

CHOCOLATE AND TOMATO GUNGE WITH FISH FINGERS IN JAMMY

RECIPE OF THE WEEK

Ingredients

~~4 escalopes of monk~~fish FINGERS
~~½ butter~~
~~2oz spinach~~ CHOCOLATE (LOTS)
~~2oz pine leaves~~ ½ TOMATO
~~1oz parsley~~ JAM (AS MUCH AS YOU WANT)
~~1 tsp Hungarian knives~~ 1 TUB SAFFRON
~~1 tbsp extra virgin olive oil~~
~~1 tbsp balsamic vinegar~~
~~50ml cream~~

(Serves ~~4~~ 1)

Separate the ~~skin from the tips of~~ FINGERS FROM THE PACKET ~~the monkfish by boiling them lightly in the butter for five minutes.~~ Chop EVERYTHING ELSE UP. ~~the spinach and pine leaves into tiny pieces, then leave them to soak for twenty minutes in the Balsamic vinegar. Clean the parsley until salt, then press into a paper. Combine the spinach, pine leaves and parsley and rub into the flesh of the monkfish until it's coated with their flavours,~~ and then place all the ingredients, ~~except the olives and cream,~~ together in a large saucepan ~~and simmer for forty minutes. Add the slices, cook for a further ten minutes, pour into an oval dish, add the cream, and serve with crusty bread.~~ MIX AND POUR INTO BUCKET AND EAT WITH A SPOON.

Eighty Five

Appendix 18

TED'S
OFFICE EQUIPMENT
Nag's Mews, Highbury, London N10

Our REF: 6387000074645T.   Your REF: 74000836310275602945710 46-04440-683585-4954-54958400B.

Dear Mr. Peen,
  Re your knackered typewriter. It's knackered mate. A total dud. Had a go at fixing yer bees and the ems starts playin the prat. Do yerself a favour and splash out on a good bit of computer kit like what I'm writin on now. People don't take you serious these days and less the words look good on the paper. I jammed down the ems but they's gonna play the prat again soon.

INVOICE

For doin the bees:	5 quid
For doin the ems:	8 quid
You owe me:	58 quid

Yours sinserely,

Ted Clapper

Edward Clapper (Managin director)

(For the purposes of keepin the books straight customers are requested to hurry up and cough up)

Appendix 19

FOR BRAINY-HEADS WHO NEED A REST FROM MY MASTERPIECE BECAUSE THEY ARE SO BRAINY.

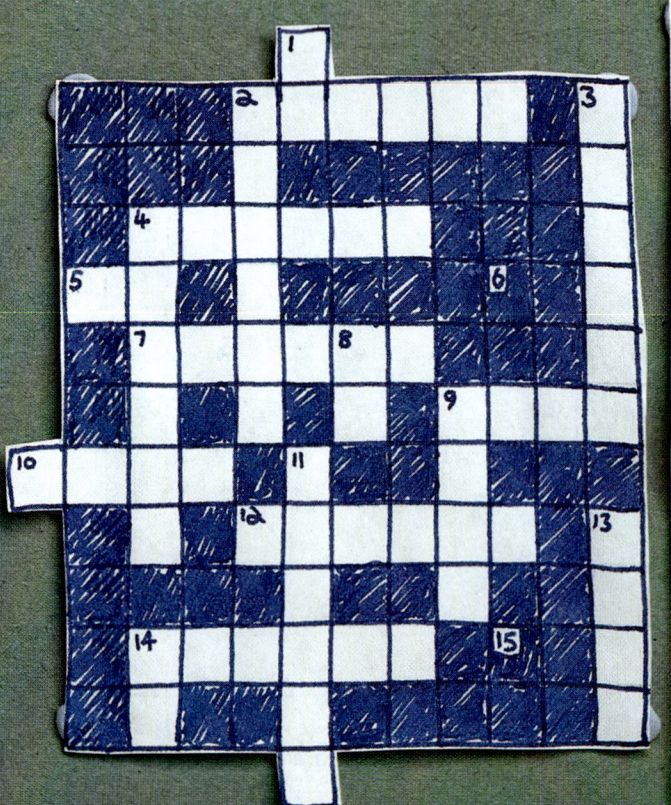

Across
2) A Gifted fellow (2,4)
4) Ban Rem! That makes an unappreciated genius (2,4)
5 and 10) Bran mixed with me produce a great thinker (2,4)
6) Nothing in these squares but darkness (0,0)
7) Talented chap in reverse (4,2)
9) This one's pulse may be a runner (4)
12) Bream N. and find a genius (2,4)
14) Mr Bean (2,4)

Down
1 and 9) Barmen make an exceptional individual (2,4)
2) Men rab to make a chap of many talents (2,4)
3) Bra man are very clever indeed (2,4)
4) Nab? R. Me creates an overlooked Brainy-head (2,4)
8 and 13) Ram Ben - shattered! Extraordinarily gifted person (2,4)
11) Bean, Mr (2,4)
14) Is he a Mrs? No, he's the opposite (2)
15) Dark squares? Yes, they are (0,0)

Eighty Six

Appendix 19b

FOR STUPID-HEADS ONLY

My masterpiece is probably going in one ear and out the other so why not do this instead?

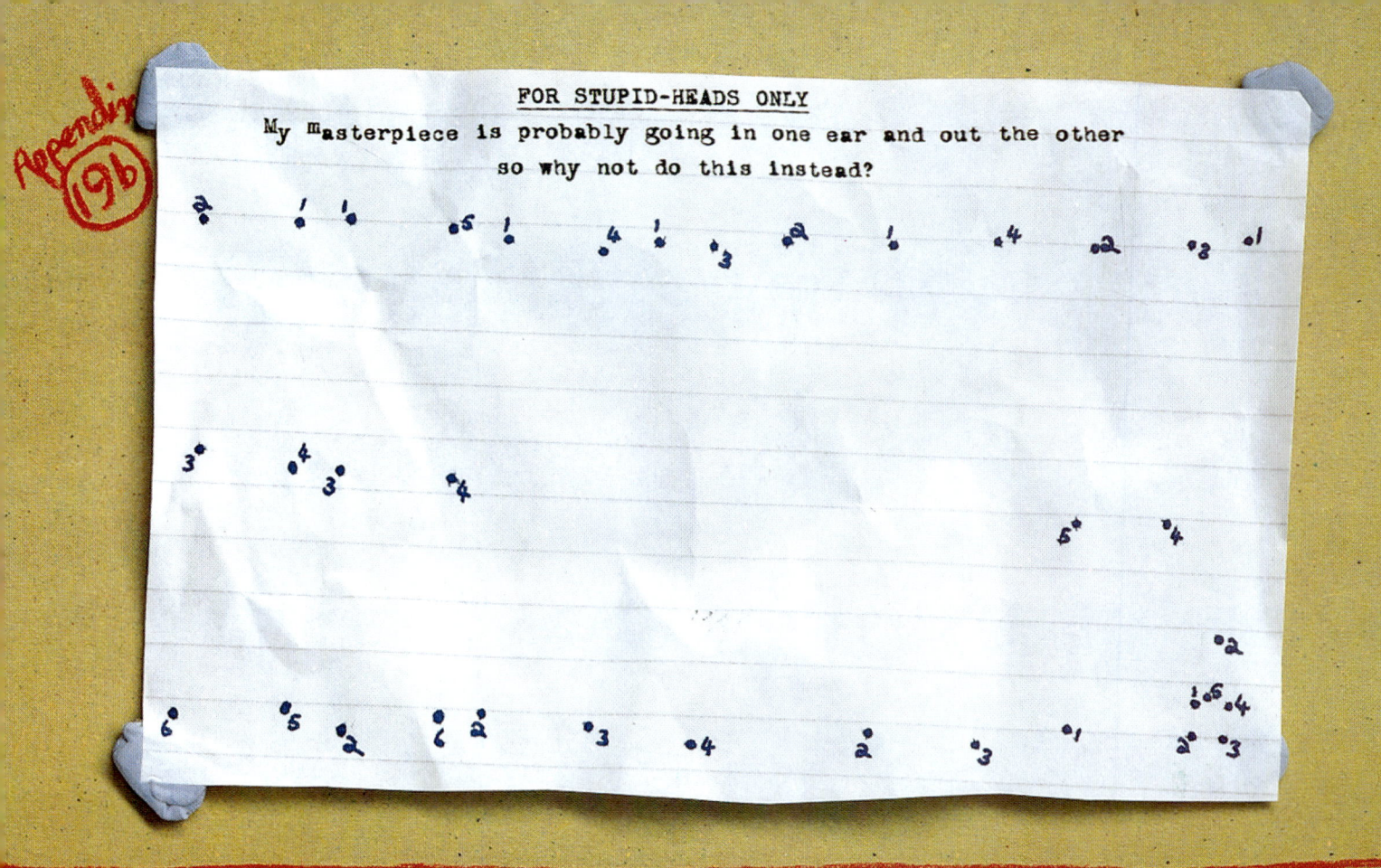

OTHER WORKS OF ART THAT I HAVE IMPROVED.
Signed Mr. Bean A.A. R.A.C. T.S.B.

Appendix 20

Eighty Seven

"Mmm... Lovely warm string vest!"

"My old man's a dustman, he wears a dustman's hat.."

Dear Mum, had a simply awful time at the barbers today-

Eighty Eight

(TEE, HEE, HEE!)

Appendix 21 EXCELLENT HANGOVER CURE
Make sure you are sitting quite near a loo and then drink all of this:

If you have drunk all of the above and there is no water trickling out of your ears then you must drink the same amount again. Don't be embarrassed. It probably didn't fill you up first time because you are fat.

Eighty Nine

Appendix 22 — Mr Bean's Guide to Dreams and their Meanings

Dreams are very odd things which tend to occur during what scientists call 'sleep'. Sometimes, they can be very loud and bright and strange, and then sometimes they can be very normal and quiet. Usually they're very well written though the ending is often very stupid. However, the wise Brainy Heads of the Olden Days millions of years ago, even before buses, used to think that dreams had special meanings, predicting the future or telling you someting you didn't already know. I agree with these ancient wise Brainy Heads and so here is my guide to dreams and what they mean.

DREAM

You are worried that the melon in your fridge is not ripe enough. Your maths teacher comes home surprisingly early and angrily asks if you have hidden a melon in his trousers. However, you realise there is a spider in the piano which might have caused both melon problems (ie, not being ripe and being in the maths teacher's tousers). You mention this to you maths teacher, holding the spider in your hand so you can see it. Then, since you are now suddenly on holiday in the South of France, he playfully pushes you into the swimming pool, laughing.

WHAT IT MEANS

This is an easy one, actually - we've all had this one haven't we (sometimes three or four times in one night)? Melon-anxieties are always to do with NOT BEING APPRECIATED PROPERLY BY THOSE AROUND YOU. The melon which is not ripe enough is like the friend who does not see what a GENIUS you are. The maths teacher with the melon in his trousers is a simple reversal - he is worried that the admiration you should be getting is actually going (unjustly) to him (all maths teachers are idiots). Spiders make webs to catch insects, including beetles. The dream is saying: if you were as admired and revered as The Beatles pop group (hence the musical reference of the piano), then you could afford to take a poolside holiday in the South of France.

DREAM

You are eathing waffles when suddenly your best friend enters and exclaims that the syrup for the waffles will be impossible to clean off the waffle iron. He offers to help you clean it, but then the waffle-iron goes missing. While you are looking for it in the clothes basket, you see in the distance out of the bathroom window a hot-air balloon with the word SNEEZE written on it. You wave to the balloon and to your amazement see that Mrs. Wicket is waving back from the balloon. You shout: where are you going? And Mrs. Wicket replies: to get some handkerchiefs.

WHAT IT MEANS

Mrs. Wicket always has too many handkerchiefs in her handbag - even if she had newmoanier she wouldn't need that many. In this dream she is clearly going to get a whole balloon basket-load of them, which is totally pointless, as she doesn't even appear to have a cold. Likewise, your best friend is worried that you won't be able to clean the waffle iron just because it's got syrup on it, which is the WHOLE POINT of waffles/waffle irons in the first place. HE is WAFFLING (two meanings of waffles, see?)! This, then, is a dream about friends who are doing pointless things and who won't listen to your advice about what they really should be doing.

Ninety

DREAM
An alligator is running after you, trying to eat you. You run up some steps to escape.

WHAT IT MEANS
You're scared of alligators. You need to take steps to cure you of this irrational phobia.

DREAM SYMBOLS AND WHAT THEY MEAN

Certain things often crop up in dreams, and they always mean the same thing. Here is my guide.

- Apples = Health (an apple a day keeps the doctor away)
- Butter = Goats (they are 'butters')
- Cheese = Cheese
- Chimpanzees = Tea
- Dad = [Research still in progress]
- Dogs = Hot dogs
- Dragons = Bad luck will be with you, in particular watch out for fires and large lizards
- Elephants (grey) = Old age
- Elephants (brown) = Poo
- Gobstoppers = Cars (possibly)
- Hot dogs = Dogs
- Kings = Prince Charles
- Lions = Prince Charles
- Lady Di = Prince Charles
- Mice = Rice
- Mum = [Research still in progress]
- Nincompoops = Poo
- Number Ninety Nine = Ice cream cornets
- Oars = Decisions to be made
- Poison = Broccoli
- Quebec = Canada
- Queues = Billiards/snooker
- Que Gardens = Cucumbers
- Red = Roses
- Roses = Strawberry creams/almond whirls
- Strawberry creams = Roses/Street
- Street = Strawberry creams/almond whirls
- Szechuan fried King Prawns with bean sprouts = Bad luck (Number 13)
- Tea = T
- Tea-bags = Bags of the letter 'T'
- Uncles = Birthday presents
- Violins = Violas
- Xylophones = Luck be with you, in particular from keyboard-based instruments
- Yellow-tinted chimneys = Beer mugs
- Zinc = [Research still in progress]

Ninety One

Appendix 23

'The Bishop's Fish' — *A Stupid book*
by Ernest P. Wicket *and greatly improved by Mr. Bean (A.A. R.A.C. T.S.B.)*

CHAPTER 1.

YUCK!

Abbot Sepelmus Crow spat a Latin curse at the moon and clutched his rich robes together against the night. His bloodied bundle bore down heavily on his shoulder, his feet unsure as they negotiated the already dew-sodden cross-paths between the graves.

He must have been a very good spitter!

The dead in this place would not bear witness against him. — *The who?* — Neither would the blackthorns that bounded the burial ground though the wind might have them flail like flags in disapproval. The boughs of the yew trees creaked in alarm, but where would they find an ear? *sheep?* In Heaven? In Hell? The cathedral spire cruelly pierced the underbelly of the moon as if pinning it in the sky, from where it's failing glow shone on the wicked crime of Abbot Crow.

Naughty!! naughty!!

Why, the cat shop of course

Sudden lightening caught his smile – a gash in flesh – as the inevitable thunder followed but moved him not. He had his prize, his treasure beyond worth, his conscience beyond redemption. He was at peace.

WASH YOUR MOUTH OUT!

Crow threw wide the graveyard gate and heaved his bloody burden towards the hogsback to the North. Into the gathering pall of the storm he strode, leaving scarlet traces in his grassy wake. They would soon be erased by God as the heavens opened and loosed a deluge of absolution. *Absolute ruddy crap, more like!*

Oh good, the hog's back. Where have you been, Mr. Hog, the loo?

Ninety Two

Things Guaranteed to Send People 'Over The Moon'

The Worst Swear-word I Know.

Appendix 25

Dear Teddy,
I expect you're getting rather thin without me there to feed you. Hold on old chum. Home soon! If the stomach gripes get too much bang on the floor. Ernest won't hear you because he's always got the telly on but at least you'll feel you're doing something useful.
Love, Beanie.

Teddy c/o Mr. Bean
c/o Mrs Wicket
'Daffodils', 12 Arbot Road
Highbury

Dear Mrs Wicket,
Howdy. Am having an absolutely splendid time in Hollywood. Had grits for lunch with John Wayne which was excellent. Only hope I've left enough room for hamburgers with Marylin Monroe at eight.
Bean.

Dear Mr. Bean,
I know you're not there because you're here but you'll be there when I get back so perhaps when I do we can read this together. I look forward to it.
Regards, Mr. Bean

Mr. Bean
c/o Mrs Wicket
'Daffodils', 12
Highbury
London N1
ENGLA

ENGLAND

Ninety Four

MR. BEAN ℅

Mrs Wicket
"Daffodils"
12 Arbor Road
Highbury
London N10

COPY FOR FILES

Miss Soames (Senior Editor)
'Boxtree' Publishers
25 Eccleston Place
London SW1W 9NF

February 11th 1997

Dear Miss Soames,

Ernest Wicket here. I am sooooooo pleased that His Highness, Lord Boxtree has recognised my genius and has gone to Australia.

I hope you don't mind, but I now think, quite frankly, that 'The Bishop's Fish' is going to be a load of crap. Instead, I would urge you to publish my latest Masterpiece: 'Mr. Bean's Scrapbook'. It is by far the most superior piece.

Do yourself a favour, Madam, and send me another advance i.e. £5000.00 and please note that I now go by the pen name: 'Mr. Bean'. (Cheques made payable to etc.)

I am, Madam, very much your own,

Mr. Bean

Mr. Bean A.A. R.A.C. T.S.B. (Novelist)

P.S. Let's get this one on the shelves before old Boxtree swans back from Down-Under, eh? And by the way, do you like my tight face?

NinetySix

BOXTREE

25 Eccleston Place
London
SW1W 9NF

Tel: 0171 881 8000
Fax: 0171 881 8001

(Twit!) →

Mr E. Wicket
'Daffodils'
12 Arbor Road
Highbury
London N10

18 January 1997

Dear Mr Wicket

I have been asked by Lord Boxtree to pass on to you his hearty congratulations on your completing the third chapter of *The Bishop's Fish*. He was, as I am, captivated!

Please find enclosed a cheque for your advance: £2,000 (contract to follow).

His Lordship will be in Australia for three months from Wednesday but he has instructed me to urge you to send us any other as yet unpublished manuscripts you may have as he is sure there is a ready market for your 'extraordinary talent'.

I await the arrival of any such document with baited breath.

Yours faithfully

Clare Soames

← *This woman must be off her RUDDY TROLLEY!*

Clare Soames M.A. B.S.C
Senior Editor

IDEA!!! →→→

Ninety Five